The Eye of the Rainbow

An Alaskan Dream and Other Tales

Ted Mattson

THE EDDIE TERN PRESS

Library of Congress Catalog Card Number 93-60206

ISBN# 0-9605388-5-2

Cover idea by Linda Ewers.
Cover design and layout by Bob Foree.
Cover art by Tom Novak.
Back cover photo by Bob Cellers.

Drawings by Diane Hill
  Eagle Creations
  8259 Juanita Dr NE
  Kirkland WA 98304

To Penny
Whose support and encouragement for my dreams never waivered. And...

For Maria
The daughter of a dreamer who, I hope, can now finally understand as her dreams in life begin to unfold.

Acknowledgements

So many people were involved in this project that it would be easy to fill pages with the gratitude I feel in their behalf. Certainly at the top of the list is my former wife Penny Mattson whose encouragement and faith in my life's efforts never diminished even though our paths parted along the way. She has always been and still remains one of my best friends and supporters.

To Whit Deschner, who ended up traveling throughout much of the book against his will, and who was there for me when it counted most I will always be grateful. He knows how to make "lemonade" from life's lemons. The week we spent together on the mountain will never be forgotten.

Faye Christensen has to be commended for her initial editing efforts and for gently guiding me around pitfalls so common with a beginning writer. She was very kind but not afraid to tell me when "omit" was the obvious choice.

To William Larned and to his son Bill who made the contact for me, I am deeply grateful. It is not everyone who gets his "wet" manuscript read and critiqued by such a distinguished reader. The encouragement was most honored.

Special thanks, too, are in order for Marilyn and Bob DeVries, and Joan Slack, for helping with the punctuation and spelling which the computer refused to find and for providing valuable feedback as well.

The computer! I thought such things were beyond my comprehension but Lesa Evers, Tom Schulman, John Salse, Judy Opperman, and Jerry Denelli took me by the hand and patiently led me through the maze until they made a believer out of me.

For Diane Hill, the artist, whose path crossed with mine in the wilderness along the Iditarod Trail in the spring of 1991, I offer my sympathy along with my gratitude. She not only brightened the pages of the book with her work, but she made working with such a critic as myself actually pleasurable.

And lastly, to all the others who took the time to read or listen to certain sections at my insistence whether for technical content or just for the feedback I needed at the time, I extend my heartfelt thanks. You all helped make this project very enjoyable.

T M

"Rainbows taken to completion are, in fact, perfect circles. It is only from the vantage point of being on earth that makes them seem otherwise. Those who fly are sometimes privileged to get a glimpse of the real thing."

Jobs are one thing. Rainbows are another. More than twenty years have passed since my wife and I, along with our young daughter, took that year off — away from the "rat race" that so many of us have been led to believe is all that life has to offer. We weren't exactly looking for rainbows, but they were there. It was the last job I've ever had.

So many things started happening to me along the way that my "joblessness" almost became a joke among my family and friends. When it looked like I was actually going to be "unemployed" forever, many of them began encouraging me to "write a book" about what was happening in my life.

And somewhere along the line, I heard myself saying: "Well, maybe I will someday."

This then is the response to the *voice* that was always tugging at me but never really telling me anything other than there has to be another way. I can not tell you that what has happened during those years was better than what may have been. But, looking back, that's the way it had to be.

chapter 1

What a stupid way to start a trip into the bush! The instant I felt the first twangs in my chest I should have stopped. No, it wasn't a heart attack. But when Frank Cranbourne started kidding Whit Deschner and me about seeing us for the last time as we hauled the gas cans out of the pick-up to top off *Baldy Bird's* wing tanks, it hit me instantly. "No," I thought, "let it go. He's always teasing and kidding around."

And so we started off. Little did we know that before nightfall, death would be a scratch away. Our plan was to scout Trail Creek, a river about eighty miles northwest of Dillingham for a possible canoe trip the following year. I'd seen the river for the first time a week or so before when I'd flown over it with another friend in his Cessna 180. It poured its crystalline water down through a sheer rock canyon wall and was fed by a number of smaller streams along its twenty-five or thirty mile run. One side stream waterfall in particular was going to warrant some exploration. The country was

spectacular! Rough jagged peaks contrasted sharply with the more typical rounded-off tops of the lower range of mountains. Snow was still hanging on in the higher peaks, but, except for the lichen patches, the August tundra was green and lush in the valleys below.

There were plenty of scud-clinging clouds near the rocks as *Baldy Bird* wormed its way up past Alegnagik and the second lake and on through the passes to the west. The blue sky we found in Sunshine Valley was more than welcome after the long stint of soggy weather we'd just experienced during our regular commercial fishing season in this southwestern corner of Alaska. We were excited to be out and doing something – a privilege not everyone gets in that remote country – as an airplane is a must.

Since Whit has about as much experience running white water as anyone I know – he even wrote a book about his adventures – I was in fine company for judging Trail Creek's canoeability.

"Ted, it looks fine but the drops are really deceiving from up here."

I tried to keep my tight turns to a minimum as I knew from experience that Whit was quite capable of chucking up his breakfast in a plane with me. It had happened before, but I was paying him back then for nearly drowning me in a Class III river. Whitney's thin strong frame fit nicely into a kayak and his dark hair showed off well the small goatee and mustache he seemed to wear as part of his clownish trademark. Today, we had no time for such foolishness. And besides, we were too many miles from anywhere to be playing around. This was wilderness. So when I noticed Whitney getting awfully quiet in the rear seat, I knew it was time to land and let his stomach settle down a bit.

"Ever pan for gold, Whit?"

"No!" he answered with more enthusiasm than I knew he had.

"Let's head over to Canyon Creek and I'll give you a lesson." I knew it was only minutes away because I'd been there in the One Eighty just weeks before. I was hoping the diversion would keep Whit's breakfast off my back seat. I didn't want to mention the airsick bags in the compartment in front of Whit unless I had to. It was better to land. As I turned *Baldy Bird* to the west, my hand slipped open the side window for the blast of cool air I knew would make him feel better.

Canyon Creek was actually a working gold mine at one time. The big hydraulic giants (water nozzles used to blast away hillsides), and steel pipes, some with water still flowing through them, and the big sluice box were all still in place. Several buildings dotted the two mile, up-hill hike to the mine itself. Everything was left pretty much the way it was when the Feds repossessed the claim a few years back. It had been in the same family since 1902, as close as we had been able to figure. There was a death in the family and the paperwork got filed late, so now this was part of the Yukon Delta National Wildlife Refuge. A sad case for the owners but a boom for recreational miners like us. It was the most exciting gold panning I'd ever found.

Whitney forgot all about his stomach when his eyes caught sight of my first pan. He was hooked as bad as I'd been many years before. And before we knew it, the long shadows on the canyon walls forced us to make a decision: Would we head back to town while there was still plenty of summer daylight left to get through the mountains or would we set up the tent and stay the night? It was an option we had left open with friends back in Dillingham.

"Don't get excited until noon tomorrow if we don't show up tonight," I'd told them before we left. "We have everything we need with us until then. So don't worry."

For the first time we noticed that our blue sky had faded considerably since our arrival that morning and we were both well aware of the weather pattern of the recent summer. It was a simple decision — we headed home.

Just as we were about to crawl into *Baldy Bird*, Whit paused to take our photo. "Better not," I cautioned." Last time I stopped to take one more photo was when Magnar and I crashed out on the beaches. It's kind of a bad omen for me."

"OK, Ted." With that we both crawled in and buckled our seat belts.

"Did you take it, Whit?" I wondered aloud after our headsets were on and the intercom working.

"No, I didn't. I believe in omens, too."

The conversation with Frank that morning flashed before me once again, and again I dismissed it as nothing. The engine started and we taxied to the up-hill end of the runway since there was no wind and did a run-up once more. Usually, I only do one in a day and let it go at that, but the right mag had been a bit rough that morning so I was curious to see if it was still the same. Now the left mag was down as well. "What the...." I mumbled aloud as I monitored the gauges.

Whit sensed my concern. "What's wrong?" he asked.

"Not sure. But we may have to stay here after all."

But then I switched from "both" to "off" a couple of times and just like that we had the RPM's we needed for take-off.

"I don't know what's going on, Whit, but it sounds OK now, so here we go." As we were rolling and bouncing down the gravel strip, the thought crossed my mind again — "Boy, this wouldn't be a very good place for the engine to quit."

But it didn't, and we churned out of there banking low over the beaver dams downstream of the strip. Then we climbed slowly up out of the valley and onto the bare slopes of the first of the mountains we had to cross before getting back over to Trail Creek. We slid along just yards above the old cat trail that led to this place from somewhere to the west. I was pumping out the last of the fuel from the belly tank as we topped the last ridge that would take us into the valley where we planned to do the canoe trip the next year. I was hoping we could get one more look at it without Whitney's stomach interfering.

It was then that I reached down and switched to the full right tank thinking it would balance our load a little better. A friend once had cautioned me to always have a forced landing area under you when you switch tanks. "That's usually when something happens — just as you make a change," he had said. And in the ten years I'd had *Baldy Bird*, I was always conscious of that advice everytime I made any changes. Except now.

It wasn't like I needed to switch tanks right then. I just did it. We had more than enough fuel in the left tank to make it the eighty or so miles back to Dillingham, but still I switched.

Never in all my days has a flying lesson been drummed into my being so deeply or into the recesses of my memory so thoroughly than at that moment on top of that treeless ridge. The engine just quit. It's one of those things you just can't believe is happening. Here we are practically sitting on top of a mountain, in an area about as ruggedly remote as you could find anywhere and the engine decides to give us a lesson in humility.

All I ever learned about flying the past twenty-five years was tested in this one single brief encounter with reality that suddenly took on the dimensions of eternity. My senses screamed at me. Everything was amplified. Where once the engine noise roared in my ears, the wind, seemingly silent before, now filled my ears as the plane plunged forward. Did it not need its engine after all? No, my insides are telling me the earth is getting closer.

I hear other noises, too. The propeller is windmilling. I see its lifeless pulsing and hear the whiffing as it is being pushed around by *Baldy Bird's* forward motion. My body senses the danger. It feels the nose down attitude, and my eyes flick over the landscape below. Fortunately, we are on the downhill side of the mountain so we have some time. Automatically, I pull the carb heat, reset the mixture and check the throttle. It is my first actual engine restart, and I am surprised at how easily it comes from my memory. The engine stays silent. Again I try the procedure, but the results are the same. Then I remember—you are to "always" switch back to your original tank. I'm irritated at myself for forgetting. When I make the switch, the airspeed indicator catches my eye. We are close to stall speed. I push the nose even closer to the earth and forget about the restart.

My internal calculators are flooding me with information. I can feel the sweat trickling down my armpits, and when I try to swallow, my mouth is persimmon juice. The smells of the cockpit are there, too. Much like they are when you open the door for the first flight of the day and reach in to check the switches and gauges. The mixture of fuel, the instrument panel, the leather seat covers, and fresh air all combine to give you the smell of an airplane — any airplane. And here they come at me again in full force. It's not an unpleasant odor, but it seems strangely out of place up here looking down at the earth instead of down there looking up at the sky. And I am aware once more of how close that earth is getting.

Every flying lesson, every hour after endless hour of practice, every book I ever read or every person I've ever talked with has not prepared me for this. I see the earth below more clearly than I ever have before. It waits with the patience of eternity. A few more seconds to it means practically nothing. To us, it could mean our lives and yet there is a calm about us. It's strange.

I've practiced forced landings hundreds of times with countless instructors over the years, and they all try to surprise their students each time they go up with them. I've even had to shut the engine down over an airfield in Canada when I lost the oil pressure. But that's just it — there was always a airfield within gliding distance. Always.

Here there are mountains and tundra but, thank God, no trees, and silently I am grateful for that. There are endless rules regarding engine failures. If you are close to the ground like on take off, you go straight ahead. No decisions to make. If you are somewhat higher and you've just taken off, you have to decide if you have enough room to turn back to the runway or only time enough to make some gentle turns to avoid any objects that may be directly in your path. But, when you are three hundred feet or so on the top edge of a mountain which in itself is a couple of thousand feet high, decisions are not quite so simplistic. They might be if you were flying someone else's bird. As friend James Clyde Spears once told me when we were flying company choppers together in the Arctic—"If this thing coughs just once, my obligations to the company are automatically terminated, and James Clyde's obligations are for James Clyde. Period!"

But this was *Baldy Bird*—my baby doll, my buddy and companion of seven trips up or down the Alcan. We'd been together ten years now. All over Alaska and across the lower 48. It was not the same, but it should have been, I know.

Somehow, my internal computer keeps functioning. But it is very apparent how an overload could short-circuit the whole thing. Fortunately, I do not panic and my senses do not let me down. I know it is not going to go well and hear myself saying: "Do what you can for yourself, Whit. It's not going to be pleasant."

He answers, his voice calm with only a hint of the strain. "Do what you have to do, Ted. It's OK." And I am thankful it is Whit sitting behind me. In his life he has known "tight" situations, too. He has kayaked over waterfalls and has been charged by an African elephant. He has known fear, and here he is the perfect companion.

The one possible place I have been eyeing on which to set us down I scrap and immediately start a gentle turn to the left knowing that *Baldy Bird* is doomed. It was an exposed patch of gravel and it had held my attention way too long. Certainly a long shot but the only area where the airplane had a chance to come away unscathed. It had a couple of bad features. There was a deep cut gouged out of its center which nearly spanned its width. I might have made it but...it had vertical walls—a dead stop! Deeply ingrained instincts said no. Possible yes, but no! The ultimate veto however was that I couldn't see over the end of the bar and I knew it could be bad down there. No, it was better to take the tundra.

"It's the 'dead stop' that kills you, Ted." Brownie's words were echoing in my head. "Whatever you do—drag out the stop. Glance off anything but keep it moving. Keep trying to fly it. What you do those last few seconds can mean the difference between living and dying."

Brownie, at 65, had survived 14 accidents flying a crop duster, and would still be spraying had he not gotten poisoned. He now worked for the cannery I fished for and we often talked flying. His words had penetrated my being nearly ten years before, and now they were back in living color. But something was wrong.

When I turned the first 90 degrees, I was actually planning a complete 180 degree turn, but now the earth was screaming up at us. And the next thing I knew we were staring into a hole in the ground. *Baldy Bird* was about to stop dead.

The next seconds bulged in my brain like a balloon about to explode. I knew I was going to die. The picture of the right side of my face and head being torn away by the engine coming through on us was all too vivid. I wondered what all my friends, whom I knew would eventually find us, would say when they saw the mess. I'd heard "pilot talk" enough to know the gruesomeness of some of the conversations.

I sensed rather than heard the deafening noise of metal tearing away from metal and the windows breaking and objects and dust flying within the cabin. I did not feel my knees penetrating the lower instruments on the panel. My left hand pulled the last of the flaps at impact because I consciously remember doing that. My right hand I have no idea about—Whitney says it was flying around with the junk in the cabin. So be it. When we hit and I pulled the flaps, I could feel us lifting back up and skidding down the slope over the tundra. Looking back, it was the big tundra tires that saved us. The reality of coming to a stop and nothing but quiet settling over us took a moment to sink in. Whit's voice came to me first. I'm not even sure what he said, but all of a sudden I knew we had to get out of there fast.

"Whit, it could still catch fire. Get out!" I yelled and immediately, without thinking, smashed out the rest of the front window. The wings had folded down around us, and I figured we needed an escape route. Whitney, not being a pilot, looked at things differently. He simply reached forward and opened the door. Both of us scrambled out from under the wing at once and stood up.

My insides were laughing—no—rejoicing. But I was numb. I think we both were. When I turned and looked at my old friend, *Baldy Bird*, my insides were sick, and I could feel the tears coming. And when it dawned on me that we were alive, they did come. Whitney walked away. His hip was hurting, but I never looked at him. I couldn't. Why men are afraid to cry in front of other men, I'll never know, but we are. The tears were stifled like so many other things had been in my life. But we were alive! There was nothing holding that back. We had survived. And now the quiet was deafening.

Slowly, we started to talk. I couldn't believe I had lost control those last twenty feet or so. The **#1 Rule** in aviation is, was, and always will be—maintain air speed. I knew it like my ABC's and yet we fell out of the sky. Yes, we were alive, but I wondered why.

Whitney, too, realized in those last seconds we were going to die and had put his head down on his lap behind my seat waiting for the impact.

"Then something told me that if this was going to be my last day on earth, then I wasn't going to miss any of it, and so I looked up," he said.

"That just might have saved you a broken neck, Whitney."

When I looked inside the cockpit and realized that I had been griping earlier about forgetting to bring the Loran C that morning, a piece of radio navigational equipment that I also used on my boat, it was apparent that its absence had also saved me broken knees. That's when I discovered the caved-in lower instrument panel. There were lots of other things bent and folded as well. All I knew to do or wanted to do was talk, and Whitney, patient as always, let me do just that.

I guess I needed to mourn the loss of my old friend. To release the feelings and somehow let it go. We talked and talked well into the night, but there was lots to do as well. Survival gear to unravel and set up. What should we do about being rescued? And always the recurring question: What about *Baldy Bird*? And so we talked and worked and took stock of what we had. A tent, axe, matches, very little food, mosquito head nets, some fishing gear, rain gear, sleeping bags, and no gun. There was a supply of bird shot for my .357 but it, too, had been left behind in the morning shuffle along with the Loran.

Since our fishing buddies were not expecting us until the following noon — a Friday — and would probably not really get too excited before that evening, we could logically not expect anyone to come looking for us before Saturday. That's when we decided to set off the ELT (Emergency Locator Transmitter) which would already have gone off had I not disarmed it. I'd been known to have a hard landing now and then, and it was easier not to have to worry about it going off accidentally.

We were still rehashing—or should I say "Ted" was rehashing—everything at 3 a.m. when we must have drifted off to sleep. I can't remember the earth under my sleeping bag ever feeling better. I was at peace with this earth. It was awesome just to be alive. To be able to see and hear and touch and smell and to wonder about it all.

It is grey and damp when morning comes. My senses are numb. Sleep has been less than refreshing. I can hardly believe what has happened. Whitney makes no movement beside me. I listen for his breathing and stay put for awhile longer, my thoughts running wild. I wonder when they will come looking for us. I can see the low clouds over the valley through the mosquito netting of the tent's doorway. It is not a day for flying. Our instincts yesterday were correct.

Suddenly, Whitney awakens with a start and sits upright! We both hear the drone. An airplane—above the clouds. Scrambling out of the tent, we run through the heavy dew soaking our stocking feet to reach the radio in *Baldy Bird*.

"Pan, Pan, Pan. This is Super Cub 679 Romeo Kilo calling any aircraft. Over."

"Super Cub 679 Romeo Kilo, this is Cessna (I miss the call sign), Civil Air Patrol out of Dillingham. Are you in distress?"

The ELT had done its job. Messages pass back and forth. We are OK. There are no serious injuries. The airplane was not so fortunate.

I heard Whitney saying: "Tell them we need some *Cutters*."

The search pilot laughed when I relayed that one. They will tell our contacts in Dillingham to send out some food, the tools we requested to dismantle *Baldy Bird*, and the *Cutters* when the weather clears.

"Is there a place to land close to you?" he asks from his perch at ten thousand feet.

"Yes, we think a Cub could land on the exposed gravel nearby."

"Roger. Good luck. Someone will come so don't worry. Oh yes — the FAA requests that you leave your ELT on during nighttime hours."

"Roger."

"Do you have an ADF (Automatic Direction Finder)?

"Yes, we do."

"You might want to monitor the regular AM frequency of KDLG's Bristol Bay Messenger at 8, 10, 12, 2, and 4 at 20 past the hour."

"We will, and thanks for your help."

"That's OK. We're glad you're all right. Good luck."

And with that he signed off. When I turned off my own radio switch, we were once again cut off from the world. We ate some of the food from yesterday, relaxed in the tent, and hung up our wet socks to dry. We were alone in this vast land with nothing to do but wait.

chapter 2

The sight of *Baldy Bird* brings back a flood of memories. So much happened to put me in this spot at this time in my life. It still amazed me that I once had a "regular" job like other folks, but that was so long ago, before that "tiny voice within" had its way. But I didn't give in easily and certainly not without a struggle. Since then, I've made my living mostly by chasing dreams. But as I said — it didn't come easily.

* * * * *

I was nearly thirty when this all started. I was sitting in a barbershop in Chaska, Minnesota in 1967 absent-mindedly paging through an outdoor magazine. My job as golf course superintendent at Hazeltine National Golf Club, with the Women's U.S. Open about to sweep us away, left precious little time for dreaming. But on my lap was a two-page layout showing a helicopter spreading fertilizer over a national forest somewhere in the West. It was a beautiful sight, and I sensed an element of excitement there as well.

"I could do that," I thought, and then realized I probably said it aloud when several pairs of eyes glued on me. No nineteen employees to look after. No one calling me on a Sunday afternoon to replace the flag on #2 green or some other equally ridiculous task. The idea of turning off the ignition key at the end of the day and having all responsibility cease appealed to me instantly.

"Yes, I could do that," I thought as I settled back into my chair once again. And a seed that must have been planted the day I was born began to stir at long last. I vowed right then to check out whatever it would take to get involved in doing that some day.

It's possible that that "Some Day" might never have come, except the next thing I knew I was flat on my back in a Minneapolis hospital with my entire family from Pennsylvania standing at the foot of my bed. Hepatitis, mononucleosis, and strep throat had me in a bad way, but I don't remember a couple of those weeks. They were in intensive care. Another month in a room and eventually a couple more months at home recuperating gives a fellow enough time to re-think some of his life.

That winter, still convalescing, my wife, Penny and I attended the National Golf Course Superintendents' Convention. It was in San Francisco, so we made a vacation of it and stopped in Oregon to visit some of her relations on the way. A helicopter was working nearby when we got to her uncle's and my attention was riveted. "Their main headquarters is right down the road." Uncle Walter said when he couldn't get me to take my eyes off it.

That afternoon, I knocked on the door of Del Smith's office in McMinnville. Del, president and owner of Evergreen Helicopters Inc., was more than receptive to an agronomist coming on staff, but he knew how to work things in his favor.

"You get your commercial-fixed wing rating first and then come back. We'll be starting a flight program soon, G. I. Bill approved, and we will train you. After that, we'll take a look at you. You'll also need to get a chemical applicator's license for Washington, Oregon, and California and do that on your own. We make no commitments."

I knew they had helicopters working everywhere, including Alaska! It was a long shot gamble, but it was a chance.

It took another year but I was back — commercial license in hand plus a wife, our three-year-old daughter, a dog and cat, all our belongings, and 2000 miles from home with no job. The tears had streamed down my cheeks when I turned in my resignation at the golf course, but all were understanding when they learned that this was my dream — a chance to go to Alaska. Only I knew that this was the longest shot of my life at best.

I was the first student at Evergreen's flight training center. In fact, I was the only student, and I was plenty scared. Somedays I could feel a vacuum pulling on me, trying to suck me back to Minneapolis and the reality of my friends and support system, which we all need. All I could do here was to physically hang onto the desk in the empty classroom until the feeling passed. But it came all too often it seemed.

The good thing was that the helicopter and I took to each other almost immediately. A love affair of sorts. I relished the flying days and looked forward to them with such increasing joy that it made those long classroom hours at least bearable, and so I managed to hang on. There was something especially challenging for me in trying to control a "bucket of nuts and bolts" all trying to come apart at the same time. And I had been right about one thing: When the flying day was over and the bird was safely back on its pad with the rotor blades secured, my day was over, too, and I could relax.

Soon I was out on my own practicing quick stops, auto rotations, hovering, and even "Whirley Bird" take-offs when no one was watching. And I loved every minute of it. The big check-ride, when it finally came, was actually anticlimatic. And so I got another rating added to my still-wet commercial license.

A lot of things were happening in the rotary flight industry during this time, but the Alaska operations always were foremost on my mind. Still I got my applicator's permits for the three states and went on the road as observer/helper/flunky and occasional ferry pilot. Evergreen was still looking at me. I'd been there nearly five months on my own before Del finally called me into his office. I was on a payroll once again.

Eventually I got to do some spraying, but the boss was always taking me on sales trips with him.

"Sales is where it's at, Ted. You could do well there," he told me.

"I guess I know that, Del, but you already have the flying part of your life out of your system. I don't."

Evergreen's Alaskan operations soon came into full swing. Oil had been discovered on the North Slope. A few of our pilots had been there, and I'd heard the talk: "Dag nab it...I ain't going back up there for nothing! No trees. Mosquitoes everywhere and zero women."

Quietly, I went home and told Penny what I planned to do. I would pack my bags and be ready to go in an hour's notice if the chance came my way. The next day I took the bag to work with me and stashed it away out in the hanger and told Fred Snell, our chief pilot, what I was doing. A month later, I was headed up the Alcan Highway at fifty feet over the trees, my fly rod securely wired to one of the

cross tubes of the old piston powered 12E I was flying with an instructor at my side. I barely had fifty hours of chopper time under my belt by then, but I was on my way.

It seems that I had been preparing for this trip all my life. But in my wildest imagination, I never considered that I'd be flying the helicopter that would take me to the place I had dreamed about since I was a boy reading Jack London and his tales of the far North. Names like Dawson, Fort Saint John, Watson Lake, the Yukon, and Whitehorse suddenly became real places. I could see how the people lived, hear how they talked, and experience what they looked at each day. I was there.

The border into Alaska deserved a photo stop, although customs for us was further up the road at Northway. We stopped anyway, along with the tour busses. I could hardly contain myself when I first stepped out onto Alaskan soil. The tourists thought we were old hands at this chopper thing — like we did it every day and they flocked over to take our pictures. We let them believe whatever they saw. But my insides were singing to the heavens and my smile for all their photos was from ear to ear. I was actually in Alaska.

In Fairbanks, after nearly seven days "on the road" as the old-time pilots call it, we met Emery. Everyone had been waiting for us and their impatience was obvious. Our client on the slope was expecting us yesterday. Still 400 miles to go. It was 9 p.m. but in June in this country, night is something you have to tape over your windows or eyes so we pushed on. This time it was Emery Lumunion who guided me along. He was an Okie, and by all outward appearances you might think he had never seen an airplane. If anything, he was the antithesis of the dashing swashbuckling pilot with whom we are so often confronted. Emery was short and scruffy-looking with a bit of a paunch. It seemed he always needed a shave, but he was probably the smoothest, most unassuming, steady-nerved pilot I've ever met. Still, he would point his face into the wind and with his big ears "feel" where the most force was coming from, and that was the direction into which we would take off.

His Okie drawl always made me smile. "Taayd," he'd say, "better use a little more RPM...yo goin' ta luse it." He was also our chief pilot on the slope and therefore was my "boss." When Emery spoke, "Taayd" listened.

At the Bettles airfield, around midnight, we topped off our fuel supply — including the extra 35 gallons we packed along on the skid racks in jerry cans.

"You can miss the stop-over at Sagwon if you want," said the FBO on the field. "It'll save you some time! Just follow the ice road thorough Anaktuvuk Pass. You'll hit the Anayoknayruk." My head whirled at the names he was slinging around. "Turn right on the north side of the mountains. Count five rivers and turn left. It will take you right to the Sagavanirktok."

Emery nodded in his slow deliberate way while his fingers followed the conversation on the wall chart in the Bettles office. I was completely lost. When we departed, it was nearly 1:30 a.m.

I never thought I could ever sleep in a chopper, but somewhere along the way, Emery took a turn driving once again. I tightened up my shoulder harness and hung my chin down on my chest barely able to keep my eyes open another second. I'd been up and going since sun-up the day before, and the thump, thump, thump of the rotor blades had pounded my body into a subconscious submission of sorts. I must have slept, for the sun was above the mountain tops, and Emery was making an approach to land when awareness returned once again.

We were above some gently rolling hills and could see off to the north. The endless lakes that characterize this land and beyond to the Arctic Ocean and the lush green of the vegetation was paramount to my senses. There was literally only the distant earth's curvature blocking our view of the tip of the world. The North Slope! The tundra I'd wondered about far too long.

"Time for gas." Emery said as we settled on to the top of a small ridge while I rubbed my disbelieving eyes yet once again.

"Where are we?" I wondered aloud.

Emery shrugged his response. "Crossed 'bout a dozen rivers so far but none looked right." Clearly, the chart indicated only five. The gas we were dumping in now would get us to the Deadhorse camp on the Sag River. It would not permit us to go searching for the gas stop we elected to bypass. It was 3:30 a.m. We snacked a bit and started off once again. Several more "rivers" passed beneath us as we made our way generally to the east—the compass no longer being the reliable instrument it was in the lower 48. Finally, in his deliberate slow drawl, "I think....maybe this here's the one," Emery mumbled aloud as he gently pushed old 63 Victor to the left, and we headed downstream toward the Arctic Ocean.

An hour and a half passed as we wound among the countless sandbars of what we hoped was to become the great Sag River. While our eyes were seeing the majestic caribou as they stomped off in their gaitly manner, our brains were somewhere between the fuel gauge and the horizon. In two hours we would be on the ground whether we were at the camp or not.

Emery's thumb slowly inched along the chart as each bend of the river became apparent. "Should be right up yonda," he said as he motioned with his head. Another minute passed in silence. And then, there it was.

I could see the blue of the ocean on the horizon as the camp huts came into view. This was the North I'd always dreamed about. My insides were shaking. I'd been in that helicopter for seven days now and nearly all of the last 24 hours. It had consumed my every moment for the past eight months, but I was there.

As we landed, Emery filled me in on some details that were not meant for "public" knowledge.

"No one needs to know ya'll only have the minimum flying time for up here. Just be careful and take it easy. Ya'll don't have to prove anything. Just fly the helicopter, and ya'll do fine. And don't take unnecessary chances. Any doubts or problems, come to me. OK?"

He reached over and shook my hand. Emery knew I was getting my big first chance to fly. I was on my own from here.

We found our way to the cook shack. Breakfast was waiting, as were my first two passengers. It was going to be a long day, but for me there was no other place I'd rather be. I had made it north at last.

chapter 3

I can't help looking at *Baldy Bird's* crumpled condition as it lies here beside us in this desolate place and wonder about the thousands of miles I must have flown over this land since that first trip North more than twenty years ago. Certainly, as anyone who flies knows, there were worse places we could be. There is a vastness about tundra that is practically incomprehensible as we sit on this lonely hillside. Even in this modern age where man flits from one remote village or camp to another in his flying machines, the size is awesome.

There is no argument that the airplane and later the helicopter changed the people of the tundra and the way life was lived here. No doubt it could be compared to the early churches and how their presence brought change to the native people that was not necessarily all good.

The arguments against the first road bisecting the last single expanse of undisturbed "real estate" in the free world continue to this minute. Real estate? The term is foreign out here. This is the land of the North. It is a fragile land and it is harsh. It is as full as it is empty.

* * * * *

I flew almost constantly after I arrived on the Slope. When I wasn't trying to catch some sleep behind cardboarded windows, I was using my fly rod somewhere or watching a grizzly bear or was trying to get close to a caribou. Other times, thousands of geese and ducks held my attention. I'd finally discovered where the geese had gone when they had flown north every spring of my life. With a helicopter at my disposal, there was no end to what I could find to do. Oh, yes—I did have to haul some people around now and then.

One evening I was coming in rather late and nearly out of gas when I spotted the first wolverine I'd ever seen. He was lumbering along a boulder-strewn river bank. Oh, how I ached inside for not having the fuel for another look, but when I landed and dropped the dipstick into the fuel tank, the ache soon changed to gratitude—I had barely a gallon remaining, if that.

Grizzly bears fascinated me the most, though. One of the first bears I ever saw was the last one I chased for photographs. I was with one of the chief surveyors when we spotted him going across a river.

"Get closer!" he shouted over the intercom, half hanging out of the door and over the skids in his excitement. Everywhere the bear went, I was there with the chopper to block his escape. Finally in desperation at this "thing" in the sky that was just beyond his reach, the bear lay down on his back and frantically clawed at the air above him. And even though we couldn't hear him, his cries of frustration and panic still echo in my ears.

It was fun following a bear's ground squirrel diggings, however. Often, as we would be flying out in the morning to the current seismic line that we were working on, someone would spot the familiar black hole against the green of the tundra where the bear had shoveled and raked out a squirrel the night before. Usually, if we were high enough we could scan the horizon and see another of the maraudings only a mile or so away. If the bear was going our way, we'd find a half dozen or more digs pretty much in a straight line. It was interesting to contemplate: Did the bear just happen upon the poor critters as he traveled along or was the wind such that he could smell his next meal from the position of his last? Regardless — eventually there he'd be, sound asleep on his back, paws flopping out to the sides in the last hole in sort of an easy-chair pose, much like my dad used to do after a big meal at home.

Once though, I got to witness a bear scooping out a squirrel first hand. He was near our Kad River camp and the guys were keeping a close watch on him through one of the transits the surveyors used. Watching his shovel-sized paws and those fixed menacing rakes, it was as though I were in the hole with him as he scooped out huge chunks of the tundra. The squirrel, scrambling to get away, was caught in mid air as he leaped from the clod of soil in the bear's monstrous paw only to have a tongue, quick as a toad's, reach out and encircle him before he disappeared inside the jaws that could crush a man's skull.

Unfortunately, camp "anti-bear" fever had been running high about this time and there was too much talk of shooting it so I convinced Vern Clamp, the camp chief, that it would be a lot less traumatic on everyone if

I quietly ushered the bear away with the helicopter. No, I didn't chase him, but he certainly moved grudgingly the four or five miles we pushed him to the south. Had we known though, we could have saved that bear a lot of grief. The next morning, there were his tracks going right through our camp on his way to the ocean beaches — the direction he had intended to go all along.

The Arctic Ocean always had me wondering about a lot of things. It was never rough and rarely was there even any sound of the surf that summer like there was on the Oregon coast. It must have been the ice pack off shore. Some days it was barely visible on the horizon and others it was within a quarter-mile of the coast line. Sometimes large chunks floating off by themselves would appear very inviting, but I always hesitated flying over so much water in a land-rigged chopper. But once when I had two guys from Arizona along, I couldn't resist any more. They wanted to be able to tell their folks back home they had stood on an iceberg in July and they planned to take photographs to prove it.

We made it out over the water OK, and I hovered over the smoothest section we could find and very gently put the skids down on the ice as they were crawling out. No sooner had their feet touched the berg when they both yelled, "Hey, you're sliding down into the water."

I had never figured on the metal skids becoming ice skates in the July sun, but sure enough, the helicopter was skidding backwards down the gentle slope into the ocean. Fortunately, I had not shut down yet so the chopper was still running, but in my panic I practically jerked the collective out of that old bird getting it airborne again. Thank goodness the engine kept up and roared to full power. As I hovered there the boys did stand on an iceberg, but they never did let go of the skids to take their picture.

Mr. and Mrs. John Allen were full-blooded Eskimos. He had worked for the Dew Line project for fifteen years before reverting back to his native life style. This was their second year of living in a tent on the tundra. They had two "eligible" daughters.

My first encounter with the Allens was when I circled back for another look at the dead caribou I had spotted on a river bank. And now that I looked around, dead animals were everywhere it seemed. Eventually I saw two people butchering one of the big bulls, and I knew they had to be Eskimos. Since I had never met a real "wild" Eskimo before, I had to land and investigate. I picked a spot which I figured was safely out of their way and shut everything down. It was awesomely quiet out there without the roar of machinery in my ears, but as I made my way to where I last saw them, the sounds and smells of nature were all around me. I was lost in my thoughts as I topped the slight rise between us, but the reality of a man coming to meet me with a gun exploded all of that.

"Oh, no—what have I gotten myself into now?" I thought, but waved and smiled my biggest smile ever. In return came a big toothless grin.

"Hello," I ventured, not knowing whether he spoke English or not.

"Hello. Where you come from?"

"From over by the Kad River seismic camp."

"Oh, I know dat place." And so we chatted awhile. When he learned that I was a "Cheechako" (one who's never been to Alaska before), he started talking about everything: How he had come to be here again after his disillusionment with the white man's society; how they lived in a tent camp nearby, but were planning to join up with some other natives who were camped a little farther to the west; and that his daughters, who had been off to school in New York for two years, were on their way home once again.

He showed me his aluminum boat, a twenty-five footer, which he had bought at a military salvage sale. It was nearly new except for a 10-inch hole bashed in the side, and "Uncle Sam" had junked it. Probably worth seven to ten thousand dollars, but he'd gotten it for a hundred, plus another ten bucks to patch the hole. It was a dandy, and John was justly proud of his prudence.

"Wanna' go for a ride in the helicopter?" I casually asked as we were walking back to where his wife was still working on one of the animals.

"This my wife Mary," John said, seeming to ignore my offer. Mary was embarrassed that I caught her with blood on her hands and dress, which was actually a cusbuk—an over garment worn by all Eskimo women. Her eyes dropped as I held out my hand to shake hers. At the same time, I re-extended the invitation to take them both for a ride.

"Too much work to do," John said. "Only I go." And so we departed, leaving Mary with the remaining two caribou.

"What are you going to do with so much meat?" I asked as we were strapping ourselves into our seats.

"Take it to Barrow in my boat. Good price! Not much caribou there." Obviously some things from the white man had rubbed off but I mentally calculated that it was nearly 130 miles to Barrow along a coast line that had "zero" facilities. If he got into trouble of any kind, he would be on his own, but I said nothing. I knew from my reading that these people were not to be underestimated.

We stopped at his camp, and he insisted on showing me his new "parky," as he called it, which his wife Mary had just completed. It was something to behold, alright, and I was mentally remembering the coy, bright smile on Mary's face, for she certainly did not have the toothless grin of her husband. She hadn't chewed these skins to softness, from all outward indications.

We were soon back at the butchering site where Mary was putting the finishing touches on the last of the dead bulls. We couldn't have been gone 45 minutes.

"How did you do that so quickly?" I asked almost incredulously. She only smiled and shrugged her shoulders. When I left, they both made me promise I'd come back again soon to have tea with them at their camp. I couldn't wait.

Throughout the summer we got to be fast friends. Whenever I was over their way, I stopped in, but usually with too little time to really visit. One Saturday I was going past them with a load and noticed that they had joined up with some other folks. Since I had to come back that way the next day, I made a midnight raid at our camp.

Seven oranges, four apples, and a six pack of coke was about all I could muster for my efforts, but when I landed and handed out the stuff, the little kids thought I was Santa Claus in a cowboy hat. This day, the Allens took "their friend the pilot" through the camp and introduced me to everyone. It was obvious my visit somehow made them important in a way I didn't understand. But since I had the time, I volunteered to take anyone for a ride in the helicopter who wanted to go. The men stoically refused—"they had seen helicopters before."

I turned to Mary. "Do you want to go? You never got a chance since I took John for that ride."

She was hesitant but excited, too. "Can Emilie go too?"

"Sure. Anyone can go!"

As the three of us started to climb in to the 12E's seats, Mary said, "Oh, wait," and she disappeared into her tent. She reappeared a few minutes later smoothing out the most beautiful, blue cusbuk I have ever seen, then or since, and she was carrying her purse.

Women, I decided then, must be universally the same. We were at least four hundred miles from a major city if you didn't count Barrow, and she wasn't going to see anyone she hadn't seen every day all that summer, but by "danged" she was going for a Sunday ride and she was dressing up for it. Purse and all.

My cowboy hat became famous that summer in a way I will never forget. I had thrown it into the helicopter at the last moment down in Oregon just so I had a broad-brimmed hat along to wear with the mosquito head net I'd packed. I was too timid to wear it in public, but it had been a gift from some real cowboys I'd gotten to know in Texas while in the army. It was a 5X Stetson, and I treasured it even if I hadn't worn it much.

I found it was great to shade my eyes with while napping in the helicopter if I wasn't flying and before I knew it, I was wearing it everywhere. And so everyone started calling me "Tex". In fact, I had the only cowboy hat I saw all that summer.

Greg, my number two surveyor, and his assistant, George, were along one day as we flew over a sizable pingo which had a family of Arctic Foxes playing around their den holes. Pingos are large frost boils that rise up out of the frozen tundra and become like large ant hill looking domes that may extend as high as forty feet. This one was about fifteen feet or so high and unusually wide. It was ideally suited for a den of foxes, but it was also an excellent triangulation point for my surveyors, so I landed.

We could see the mother fox barking at her kits, forcing them into the den, but she stayed and stared at us from the entrance. I walked over for a closer look while Greg and George set up the transit. Outside the den were several partially decomposed lemmings — the first I'd ever seen, but I had read about their supposedly mass suicide migrations to the sea. The vixen had backed away as I got closer, but she never took her eyes off me for a second. I wondered how deep into the den the kits had gone, so I lay down and stuck my arm in up to my shoulder. The next thing I knew, I had an excited mother fox barking in my face as I tried to scramble out of there. Somewhere behind me I could hear Greg and George laughing.

Well, I wasn't about to be outdone by a fox, so I lay down again and stuck my arm down the hole once more. This time when she came at me, I took my Stetson off and swished it in her face which only made her jump back a bit. The more aggressive I was, the bolder she became. Since there was no way for me to relax feeling around in the den entrance with her snapping at my face like that, I got to my knees. When I did, she scampered back about ten feet but kept her eyes glued to mine. On an impulse, I took the hat and threw it at her thinking she might run off and leave me in peace. After all, I had no intention of harming her babies. But instead she stopped, looked over at the hat, then looked back at me, then back at the hat.

I was dumbfounded at what happened next. Before I could react, she pounced on my treasured 5X, grasped it in her teeth, and trotted down off that pingo quick as that.

"Hey! You get back here!" I yelled. But she never missed a beat and all I could see was my hat nearly hidden by the tall grass, slowly loping farther and farther away from me. George and Greg were rolling on the ground with laughter by this time, but this was serious.

"Come back here!" I screamed again.

The helicopter was still running, and I was about to head for it when I saw my hat stop. It was maybe seventy yards out by then, but I could see the pointed ears of the fox's head peeking up from behind one of the grassy hummocks, and again her eyes were fixed on mine. I wasted no time getting down off that pingo and tearing out across those tall swampy tufts of grass, water flying everywhere. I would be damned before I was going to let a fox get away with my hat. As I got close to her, she turned and trotted off leaving it where she stopped. But she had the last word. My nearly new 5X Stetson lay there, right side up, its brim filled with fox pee.

For a moment I was stunned and then started to laugh. By now Greg and George were beside me, and we all laughed until tears streamed down our cheeks and our sides ached. Today, the smiling tears still come when I think back to that mother fox who must have written the book about "out-foxing" the enemy.

No matter where I went on the slope that summer, the "moccasin telegraph" had preceded me. If I had on my Stetson, I was known. "Oh you must be the guy that had the fox pee in his hat." I'd just smile.

There were some serious times on the tundra that summer as well. Not long after arriving on the Slope I was asked to do something I had only minimal instruction in before leaving the States. Lifting an "external" load was something helicopters did very well, but it took practice. My "practice" had consisted of lifting a fuel drum — twice.

We were out on a seismic line which is what oil companies use to determine what is actually "down there" before they drill. The technique usually involves drilling a series of holes down into the earth deep enough to get under the permafrost. In some cases as much as a thousand feet to get below the frozen surface. Explosives are then placed down into the holes which are then simultaneously blown so the shock waves can be recorded and analyzed at computer centers down in the States. It is a very complex and time-consuming process and the oil companies were always searching for ways to simplify the whole thing and hopefully do it faster and more economically.

One such technique involved what they called "thumpers," very sophisticated gas-filled guns or cylinders which sent an eight to ten inch ram jolting into the ground with terrifically sudden impacts. Seven of these contraptions were very accurately spaced along a row and then charged with the explosive gas. They were then set off simultaneously with radio signals, and the resultant shock waves analyzed as before. No drilling was involved at all, and the technique was extremely fast.

However, all of them had to be working and one of ours was acting up. I had just brought a technician out to see what was wrong. The whole crew was idle because of the malfunction and were standing around swatting mosquitoes and complaining. Rather than stick my nose into what was happening, I settled myself down inside the warm bubble of the helicopter to continue reading *Cheyenne Autumn* away from the mosquitoes, which were always the worst on calm days. Soon there was a knock on the bubble.

"Can you give us a lift?" the technician was saying.

"Sure, what do you need?" I answered, wondering why the half dozen guys standing around couldn't handle it.

"We need you to lift the ram out of the cylinder with the chopper."

I swallowed hard. Emery was seventy miles away on another job so I had the only helicopter available. It was a bad situation but unavoidable.

"O...K..." I said as slowly as possible, trying to find the time to think.

"You give me the signals and I'll follow your lead." It was all I knew to do. My instructor had gone through the routine with me in the States. I hoped these guys knew the same sign language.

When you are lifting an external load, since everything is happening under the center of the helicopter, all the pilot can do is watch the ground person for his clues on which way to move the chopper. I was glad it was calm. Hovering dead-center over any object is difficult enough without having to contend with the wind as well.

I moved the 12E ever so cautiously — its screaming blades gratefully thrashing the mosquitoes away from the crew who had now become the on-lookers and were watching the show. My eyes were riveted to the technician's hands. If he gently pointed to the right (his left), I inched my way to the right. Slightly up and I barely increased the pressure on the collective. Now, he was motioning me up. Still up. Higher yet. I was twenty feet or more above his head and was glad he kept backing up so I could keep him in full view. My palms were sweating through my leather gloves, and now I knew why all working pilots wore them.

"Over to the right. More right. Further still. Now down. Gently. Down some more. Hold it."

I listened through his hands.

"Cut."

He gave me the universal sign of his finger across his throat to separate the load from the helicopter. My thumb ever so softly resting over the red button on the cyclic now punched it down. I was home free. He motioned me to land back over to where I had started.

"Whew." I thought. "I scraped through that one." Soon though, I settled down to my book once more. I must have dozed off as the adrenaline rush subsided because another rattling on the bubble brought me up with a start.

"We need you to lift it back in," he was saying this time. "It's all ready."

The thought never occurred to me that they would be putting it back together today. Maybe tomorrow, after we had taken it back to camp and had it repaired in the shop. Then I could get Emery to arrange to have me somewhere else, and have a more experienced pilot come back here to finish the job.

"It's fixed already?" I heard myself saying in disbelief, wishing I could crawl into a hole somewhere.

"Yep, let's go."

I could have told him I wasn't qualified and that what I'd just done was mostly luck, but it would have sent more repercussions down the line than I was prepared to handle, so I fired up old 63V once more. This was one of Evergreen's original helicopters and it had seen plenty of work.

"Come on old girl, you can do it," I said, trying more to bolster my shaky confidence than anything else.

I followed his every minute signal. This was a piston being shoved back into a cylinder — piston rings and all. The tolerances were beyond comprehension and lowering one into the other in the field like we were was a deliberate gamble against the clock. Even with tons of experience, one slightest wrong move, a wind gust or anything, could upset the whole procedure — even damage the precious gun. And I knew that men were working directly under the chopper, innocently risking their necks, trying to mesh everything in place in one last ditch effort to get the line operational again. The big oil lease sale was getting closer and every minute meant more information would be available as to what was in the ground before the bidding started.

The cylinder and ram went together on the first try and I could sense the clapping of hands around me as I got the signal to cut it loose. I set the chopper down in disbelief. Everyone was smiling and scurrying about, glad to get on with it. My insides were shaking. This time I got out and found a bush. Pepsi never had *anything* over that pause that refreshes.

As the summer progressed, my confidence grew. Emery and I were together once in one of the big 205's (better known as the Huey) when we got trapped in fog. We had just picked up the crew and it was time to head home when we saw it rolling in from off the coast. Emery had been letting me get a little turbine time in on the side. Soon it was zero, zero. Meaning we couldn't see forward, backwards or up. We had the options of spending a soggy night with no provisions, or relying on Emery's ingenuity and experience to get us out of there.

We all looked at the topographical chart the surveyors used which had all the completed seismic lines plotted. It looked more like a city map with all the crisscrossed lines on it. We were about twenty miles from home or at least where one of the lines crossed the Kad River a few miles south of camp.

"If we could find that line..." Emery said in his drawl now familiar to everyone as his finger went slowly over the map. "We could be back in time for supper."

I knew from flying the lines with Greg how they were set up. Each quarter-mile was marked with a piece of lath driven into the ground with brightly colored ribbons tied to its top. Between each two laths were three equally spaced little flags attached to wires like you might see marking buried power lines in the lower 48. I'd watched the chain crew mark out these lines, and knew they were as straight as a bullet could fly. The question was — could we fly in this fog?

"You drive, Taayd," Emery said as we loaded the crew. He had a way of teaching that was straight to the point. "Now hover over there and set her down." He pointed to one of the ribboned stakes. "What does the compass read?" He was all business as he spread the surveyor's map out on his lap.

"About 105 maybe slightly more."

"OK — hold that heading and let's start. Take it easy and stay right close to the ground."

And so into the fog we went. One of the little flags went skimming underneath. A couple of seconds later, another. I could hear Emery counting quietly to himself. "One thousand...one, one thousand...two, one thousand.... flag. One thousand...one, one thousand...two, one thousand... stop."

I set it down and Emery climbed out and walked around and around the helicopter in the fog. When he climbed back in he told me to hover over to my left a little bit and sure enough another tiny flag was there. "Go." he said. "And keep that heading."

Pretty soon it got to be a rhythm of sorts. The counting, the flags going by, the stake. Over and over again. Each ribbon was another quarter-mile and they were going by rather regularly. "Stop." And the whole procedure would start again.

They had to heat up the supper for us but it sure beat sleeping with the mosquitoes as the sad looks on the faces of the Vertol crew indicated when they rolled in the next morning. As much of a confidence builder as it had been, it didn't even come close to preparing me for nearly losing an engine soon afterward.

In early August, we were fighting a spell of bad weather. Snow blanketed the tundra. Bear tracks were easy to spot and the Canada geese were nervously lining up by the thousands on the ocean beaches for their flight to warmer weather and the guns that waited them en route.

Our work had taken us progressively west from the Kad River camp to which we had moved after Deadhorse, and now fuel had to be moved out to strategic locations throughout the area to keep us operating. I had landed at one of these gas caches one miserable morning and the wind decided to pelt my face with the icy snow that had been blowing around for a week by then. I just snuggled a little further back into my fur trimmed hood and kept pumping.

All aviation fuels are color coded, and it was a company policy to filter everything that went into the fuel tanks, so there really was no excuse for what happened. The filtered funnel I was using seemed to take forever to let the fuel into the tank but I attributed that to my impatience because of the ice crystals that were trying to force their way into my cheeks and eye lids. I probably should have noticed the color as well but when you take the seal off of a barrel stamped 100/130 octane AV GAS, 100/130's what you expect to get. Mistake number two.

I fired it back up and took off across a mile long lake, glad once again to be inside the cozy bubble. The wind was frothing the surface of the water below me. John, the explosives man, motioned me off as I was about to set down near one of the drilling holes he was filling with dynamite. I was about fifteen feet above him and so just slid the bird sideways a bit to position myself further from where he was working on the lake shore. As I began to gently set it down amongst the hummocks, the old trusty 12E just fell out from under me. The engine was running and I attempted to pull on full power but there was no response. We hit the soft muskeg and snow with a splat, the skids hitting exactly the only level spot there.

I was in one piece but I figured the helicopter was not and tried to shut it down to have a look around but the engine refused to quit. I pulled out the mixture but instead of stopping it ran faster. Finally, I killed it with the mags and got out. Miraculously the chopper was fine but I couldn't figure out the engine acting the way it did and radioed back to camp for a mechanic to come out.

Tim questioned me over and over. "Now go through that again. You were hovering and it just fell and then it wouldn't shut off?"

"Yes, that's what happened."

By now several hours had passed and I was getting chilled. A fire was always easy when you had a metal match and some AV GAS. The intense spark was possible in any weather and a tuft of tundra grass with a little added petrol made an instant fire.

"Hey, it didn't light." I said aloud in disbelief.

"What didn't?" Tim said over his shoulder as he was fiddling with something on the carburetor.

"The gas I just drained from the engine sump."

Tim was there instantly and even John came over. "Do it again," he said. So I struck the metal match once more and the shower of sparks rained down on the fuel soaked grass without a response. Tim lit a wooden match and held it to the tinder. Slowly the fire spread and the grass hummock turned to flames, black smoke billowing down wind.

"Where did you get this fuel?" Tim was now draining one of the sumps into a juice can.

"Across the lake. I just took it out of a sealed 130 octane drum. Opened it myself."

"Well, it's stove oil."

And now the slow funnelling, the odd color and even the trouble I had standing the barrel upright to install the pump all came back to me. My knees got rubbery when I thought of that frothing lake I'd just crossed.

As soon as I found Emery, we started reviewing auto rotations—"real ones." In my training, no one had

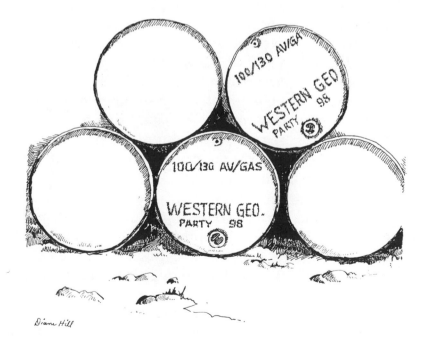

let me go all the way to the ground. Emery shut the engine off at about a thousand feet. As I said—he didn't take any short cuts.

I found four more barrels of fuel oil that summer. All were marked 100/130 Octane AV GAS.

Fishing took up a good portion of my time when I wasn't flying. Both are well up on my priority lists. The char were turning bright orange by now as the season wound down and they were absolutely wild on either fly or spinning gear! They were the first fish I'd ever caught that made me gasp in excitement.

Three of us were heading to the coast fairly regularly these days, usually with an excuse to go check on something, because then the company for which Evergreen was working had to pay the flight time. After supper was the best time to go. We even brought enough back to have a fish fry for the whole camp (over a hundred of us) so our activities were pretty well known. A well placed bribe never hurts.

John, the powder monkey, had an afternoon off so I managed to take him over there early one time thinking Greg and I would come over later with our regular after-supper excuse to go check on something. As we were loading up, one of the drillers came along with his fishing pole in hand.

"Oh come on. Please take me. I'm going home tomorrow and I haven't gotten to fish once all summer."

"Look. There are only three seats in this thing and I already have a guy over there. I just can't make an extra trip for you. It's hard finding enough legal reasons to go as it is."

"That's OK, I don't have to sit in a seat. I'll ride in the cargo racks on the way home."

I just couldn't leave him, so now there were four of us enjoying an arctic evening in the land of the midnight sun. When it finally was time to leave, the driller never hesitated and lay down in the empty rack, pulling his hood up over his head.

"Here, let me tie this rope around you at least. I don't need you rolling off somewhere along the way."

Emery was standing there when I landed but he patiently waited until the others departed.

"DON'T EVA LEMME SEE YA'LL DO THAT AGAIN!" And then more calmly: "The FAA would have a picnic looking through the wreckage of a three place helicopter and finding four bodies." I know......when Emery spoke, "Taayd" listened.

By that fall, I had logged nearly 500 hours of helicopter time and realized I was just then beginning to learn about flying.

chapter 4

There is a forlornness here on this mountainside amid the debris of the crash and our little camp. Whitney and I expect herds of caribou to be moving through the valley below or on the distant hillsides but find only a few partially buried antlers of migrations long past. In good years on the well-drained soils, the tundra crowberries, which the Eskimos call blackberries, cover the ground in patches amidst the lichen and reindeer moss. And blueberries can hang thick from their tiny bushes that tower over the dwarf willows underfoot. Lingonberries, too, can be found, their bright red "unripeness" smacking of holiday fare yet to come.

This is only a moderate year, and Whit and I have to search for the best areas where our pail can be filled. The gathering has a rich fullness about it though, and we find a certain contentment on this lonely hillside so far from civilization.

It has been better than twenty years now since, on a lark, my wife and young daughter and I "dropped out" and went to live on that little farm in northern Wisconsin. There, the blueberry and raspberry picking never seemed to end. And there was a certain satisfaction about being there that was never anticipated. For a year we sat back and let the world rush by. It changed my life forever.

* * * * *

The transition from the helicopter "rat race" to the farm came suddenly that November. I terminated myself from the second major job of my life but it was a friendly departure. Adjusting to the new pace was quite another matter. We moved back from Oregon and into my wife's Aunt's place, the house faded now to a dull red from the years she had been a widow. Leaving to spend a year with her children, the place was ours. It nestled nicely among the maples and elms and some spruce on a slight hill and back from the gravel road more than a quarter mile. Gravel? I had never lived on an unpaved road before.

It was nice on the hill amongst the trees. The summer breezes kept the mosquitoes at bay and it was cool and refreshing. In winter we were snowbound as often as not, but it was cozy and warm. There were tons of projects that needed doing, however, in a house that had been neglected so long. And some needed doing right now. In fact there were so many we wanted to do, that if we weren't careful, the year we planned to spend as recluses in this little northern community would surely go by without our ever having the chance to experience the laid-back life style of which we'd dreamed so often.

Little did I realize that when I went in to Schraufnagel's Hardware and Lumber Supply, clutching

Diane Hill

the lists I'd so methodically laid out for all the projects we'd planned, I'd get a new meaning for the term "laid back."

"What do you mean you don't have staples? When are you going to get them?" My ears were still ringing from the clerk's calm announcement that they were out.

"Well, when are you going to get them?" I asked again, my voice sounding a bit shaken by this time.

"Oh, maybe next week or the week after. Whenever the truck gets here." His slow, calm voice was as matter-of-fact as if this were an everyday occurrence. And then in his Upper Peninsula, Northern Wisconsin accent he added, somewhat more jovially, "No use worrying. Can't do anything about it, eh?" And then it hit me: No, I couldn't.

I was smiling as I drove back to the farm with what supplies they did have. There, I propped my feet up on the wood stove and sipped on a cup of coffee. Obviously I needed to re-think this year that was laid out before us. Fresh out of the second job I ever quit in my life, and unlike the tears that were streaming down my cheeks the first time, I was whistling going out the door this time. What a marvelous feeling to have that much control over your life — but scary too.

Our daughter was nearly five. We had three thousand dollars saved up, and six months of unemployment coming, and a place to live for a year. What more could one ask for? This was 1969. Thanksgiving was fast approaching and we had lots to be thankful for, and so we settled down and relaxed like everyone else had learned to do in this crossroads community.

Sitting at the kitchen table one morning, we saw a deer walk through our yard. Hunting season was in full swing then, but for some reason I was content to be there watching instead of participating in the hunt. A first in my life. Was I getting too old? No, something inside me was satisfied and very peaceful. Later in the year I would discover my outdoor magazines, piled in a corner—the endless subscriptions unopened and unread. The need for them no longer existed for me. I wasn't in a cage looking out anymore. I was free. Well, almost anyway.

We still had to eat and had some bills. Electric and telephone mostly. The car and truck, too, so we jacked up the car and left it for the winter. We would only need the pick-up. Our lifestyle slowly molded around what we had and not what we craved. Fortunately, we had no debts, a lesson my father unknowingly drummed into me. He paid as he went. I can remember wanting a bicycle so badly I dreamed of it at night and was envious of the other kids riding theirs, but eventually it came. I had learned early about waiting and now found it not nearly as disagreeable as I imagined in my youth. We could plan our lives because we were not chained to the grist mill. Most of our neighbors here governed their lives as well. It was a delightful change from the real world. Or maybe this *was* the real world. There would be lots of time to think about that one as the year progressed.

The library became the mainstay of our entertainment. Our weekly trips to town always were planned with time to spend browsing. We would come home with our groceries and having done our errands, with piles and piles of books and then spend the week drooling over them. Reading to our daughter and reading to ourselves got sandwiched between keeping the woodpile stocked, thawing the pump in the springhouse and shoveling out the path to the small barn which housed the rabbit hutches. Why does everybody think some rabbits would be nice? I got very involved too quickly.

"How-to" books were my favorites that winter. It was fun to see something in a book and then set about doing it, which was how the thing started with the rabbits. But there was also soap and cheese-making, candles to try and eventually maple syrup to boil when March finally blew in. Endless hours of pleasure from both the doing and the reading how.

The rabbits, though, took the most time but they were Maria's favorite. She loved to be out helping Daddy in the barn. And she learned that eating the rabbits was also part of bringing them into the world, although I tried to do the butchering when she wasn't around.

Hormel came into our lives not long after reading *Charlotte's Web*. A neighbor asked us if we wanted him. The runt of the litter and unable to compete for a teat of his own, Hormel was soon greedily slobbering down bottle after bottle of warmed milk. He followed us everywhere and was soon running out with the dogs to greet whoever drove into our driveway. Then one of us would have to tear out there and save the helpless victim from being showered with pig kisses. Hormel loved to jump up on his hind legs and be greeted and petted like the dogs. Dogs can be careful about jumping up on you, but pigs know no such bounds. When he decided to plow up the grass in the entire yard one warm spring afternoon while we were in town, his freedom days were numbered, and he eventually had his own pig pen. The following autumn Maria was told the day before butchering. She had known from the start that the best we could do for Hormel was to give him a fantastic six months of life. And that's what we did. He was lavished with love and loved us in return. But it was not the best pork we ever ate.

Milking Sarnstrom's cow and feeding their beefstock for two weeks we did as a gift to Joyce and Earl, our neighbors across the fence. They wanted to go down state to visit her parents for the two weeks over Christmas and take their kids along.

"Sure we can do it," I volunteered. "Penny used to milk when she was a kid. She can show me how. It'll be fun. Don't worry about a thing," I said, mustering all the reassurance I could.

But deep inside, I didn't have much of a fondness for cows. And certainly — I was not aware that our newly acquired laid-back lifestyle was about to be field-tested almost beyond repair. Caring for rabbits, two dogs, a cat and a pig was one thing. Cows were another matter entirely.

The half-pail of milk didn't seem like much at first. You would think the rewards would be somewhat greater coming from an animal six times our size. Couple that with the work of dragging the hay down from the loft and shoveling out the manure from the stall into a wheelbarrow, and then precariously balancing your way along the narrow boardwalk over the heap of dung to dump the steamy load in the frosty air with your nostrils and lungs stinging from the urea smells, and you have some idea. Unfortunately, the work was just beginning.

The procedure was to put the milk in Joyce's refrigerator after straining it, to let the cream rise and of course we were to use all we could ourselves. The first few days went fine but a half pail grows to a full pail at the end of the first day. By three days, it's grown to five gallons or more and we were drinking all we could get down at home.

And so it was butter in the blender from the cream. Then a trial with cottage cheese and a cooking thermometer in a huge pot of the clabbered milk trying to raise the temperature one degree per hour until the correct consistency was reached. It was a task I found nearly impossible and only once did a product emerge that even closely resembled the store-bought variety. But my Scottish side persisted and I was loath to waste anything. Even Hormel couldn't keep up with the bounty from one cow. And then when something good did come off the stove, I was reluctant to eat it because it might never happen again.

It was not hard to make "squeaky cheese" though. A favorite with all the Finnish relations in the area. Just clabber the milk with a rennet tablet from the drugstore or farm supply house and squeeze out all the whey through double cheese cloth and press the curds into a flat glob which usually fit on a large dinner plate — the end product from one milking. Toasted under the broiler with a little sprinkling of salt, the new cheese was a favorite anytime. But even a good thing gets to be too much after a while.

So I tried to make real cheese — aged and everything. "After all, this was the 'dairy state,' was it not?" I reasoned with my wife as I was trying to borrow the only two of her stainless steel pans that fit inside each other.

The press was the main problem as I saw it, but the car jack between two closely spaced trees and the pans solved that, or so I thought. The cheese was only marginal, but the pans never survived the pressure and I heard about that all winter.

In our two weeks as real farmers, we had more butter than we could use in a year. We had made and eaten more ice cream than anyone needs — ever. And none of us could stuff down another piece of that squeaky cheese. It was with great pleasure that we watched the lights come on that night at Joyce and Earl's when they finally came home. Tomorrow, we could sleep in.

Mornings were my favorite time of day except when we were "farming." I liked to get up before everyone else and stoke up the fires in our two woodstoves. Soon the coffee would be ready and the sourdough biscuits were set to rise in the warming oven. This was my time, and I liked to bury my nose in one of the many books we all had going at once. With my feet propped up and sitting in the rocker with a coffee cup nearby, daylight would often catch me by surprise.

When the biscuits were high, I'd put them in the oven and set another pot of coffee on the stove. Penny loved to be awakened by the smells of the freshly baked breads, dripping in butter (our own) and the coffee filling the room. It was a good time in our lives — probably the best.

Later, towards spring, making maple syrup became a close second. Pouring the delicious homemade golden syrup over flapjacks has no equal. There were some giant hard maples on an abandoned farm nearby and when the snow started to melt in March, I gathered together the materials I was going to need: Five gallon lard pails from the bakery in town, spouts which I managed to borrow, a pan that I had to have made at the last minute, an old stock tank that I converted into an outdoor cooker and some ten gallon milk cans to haul the sap home to where I'd assembled a stove of sorts out by the barn and handy to the wood pile. It was easier to do the cooking close to home than out in the woods like was done in the larger "sugar bushes."

Ours was a small time affair, but the six gallons of finished syrup we made was no small thing. Almost a 55 gallon drum of sap had to be boiled away for each of those gallons, and I learned the hard way not to scorch the pan, for it took eight hours of sanding to get rid of the burnt sugar. It was then I started bringing the nearly finished syrup into the house and watched the thermometer closely until it finally reached 7 1/2 degrees above the boiling point of water, at which time the sap is officially pure maple syrup.

Beyond that you can make candy and even maple sugar, which we tried as well. It was lots of hard work, but we were finding that was the way it was among these out-of-mainstream so-called laid-back northerners we had joined for a year.

It wasn't all work, though. Snowshoes and cross-country skis found lots of use. Sometimes I'd go out in my winter whites and ski the snowmobile trails. It was amusing to move just off the trail when I'd hear the distant drone of a string of machines coming my way. I'd stand there, perfectly still, and they'd come whizzing by one after the other, sucking in each other's exhaust, the stench of which lingered long among the balsams and birch after they passed. No one would notice me at all, and I wondered what they were looking at in their travels?

Off the trail, snowshoes were best. Once when I was out with Buff, our yellow lab, he started raising quite a ruckus down over a steep ravine which I hesitated to negotiate, strapped into the webs like I was. By the time

I got them off and slid down over the hill on my rump, Buff's barking was somewhat subdued, and it took me a little while to realize he was down under the bank by an overturned spruce tree just upstream. I pushed my way through the drifts, hoping I'd get there before he got a snout full of porcupine quills—which was about all I could figure was this far out in the woods that he would be that excited about.

When I got to him, only his tail was sticking out from under the hole beneath the spruce, so I grabbed it and started pulling him back out toward me. He was really furious and nothing I said would calm him down, and yet he had no quills sticking out of his face or anywhere else that I could see.

"What in the world are you so excited about, Buff?" I said as I tried to peer into the blackness of the hole, which I could now see had been enlarged considerably and very recently. Buff kept trying to lunge past me, barking and now almost frothing at the mouth.

"What is it, Buff? What's in there?"

Lying down, I squirmed my head and shoulders into the darkness, Buff still clamoring to squeeze in as well. When my eyes adjusted, I could see the hole turned to the right slightly and so I wiggled my 190 pounds in a bit farther. Now it was really dark, and when my eyes focused this time I was staring right into the face of a—wolf? "No," I thought, "It's a pig." A wolf would have been on me already. Its big nose was just inches from my face. "But what's a pig doing clear out here?" My thoughts were racing now.

Then it started chomping its teeth together, and I knew I'd made a big mistake for I was staring face to face with a bear in his own den. Buff was still frantically trying to claw his way in there beside me, barking even more excitedly than before. But now I was frantically trying to get out of there; and every inch I went backward, Buff got closer. Finally though, I was able to grasp his collar and pull him out with me, and together we slid down onto the ice on the stream below the den. I had to get my belt fastened to his collar as a leash because there was no reasoning with him. He just wasn't going to quit. Eventually, I got the snowshoes back on and practically had to drag the dog more than a quarter-mile from there before he calmed down and we could head back to the farm. The snowmobilers never got a chance like we just had.

Next day, I told Russell, our bachelor neighbor on the other side of us, the whole story.

"I don't understand it," he said, "I've been here my whole life and have never even seen a bear. You're here a couple of months and get to crawl into a den with one." He was shaking his head in disbelief.

"Better be careful who you tell, though," he continued. "There are enough outlaws around here that would go there and dig it out and kill it."

Later that spring, Buff and I hiked back over to that valley to check on the den once more and ran across fresh bear tracks. By then I had learned at the library that black bears are one of the true hibernators and don't wake up easily from their winter's nap. A good thing. We left the area knowing they sometimes return to the den after having a look around and resetting their snooze alarm. There was still way too much snow to get excited about getting up yet, and I was glad he was still safe and smiled to myself thinking of how close we'd been. He'd probably be a nuisance come berry-picking time, but he probably thought the same about us.

Not long after the sap stopped running in the maple grove, it was smelting time on Lake Superior. The big lake was a drawing card for folks as far away as the Twin Cities when the smelt started running. There was a carnival atmosphere along Ashland's lake shore, with dozens of campfires flickering into the night to ward off the winter chill still coming off the lake. I should have realized the washtubs of smelt we saw in various pick-ups going south to the cities would be divided among lots of families. The washtub I lugged home about killed us. We cleaned smelt all the next day and into the night. Fresh, frozen, or pickled—we couldn't eat any more or give it away. It was another of those lessons learned the way you never forget it. Like the garden.

"Ted, we don't need three dozen tomato plants!" Penny cautioned as I transplanted the last of the seedlings into their individual containers.

"But the rows will come out even." My logic obviously going over her head. It was the same with the beans, turnips, peas, broccoli, cauliflower, squash, (4 kinds), rutabagas, sunflowers, potatoes, onions, dill, eggplant, and peppers.

Russell had let me borrow his tractor and disk to work up the garden spot. Unfortunately, it was much easier to work up and plant than to keep weeded. Soon our laid-back days were turning into work days, however pleasant, but it really didn't matter. Everyone worked hard around there it seemed.

Working was one thing—a job was something else. The difference I learned many times over during that year we dropped out. Working was something you did because you liked it or wanted to. A job was something you *had* to do, usually because someone else was demanding it, and that could even make it worse. I did wish I hadn't planted so many tomatoes though, because by June, I realized I wanted to fly once again. I could feel it in my bones, and I knew it was time for Ted to go back to work.

Penny, congenially, agreed to keep the garden weeded, providing I was back in time to help can the tomatoes. I would only be gone from home for the summer. Home.... the word was strange to us in a way. We hadn't been there quite a year, and yet in the first seven years of our marriage, we had already lived in seven states and eleven houses. But now we were home. It was strange. Penny's aunt decided to stay a second winter near her grandchildren. "Would we mind staying on?" Amazing how things work out sometimes.

Maria would be starting school that fall. Our life was beginning to fall into place.

chapter 5

When Whitney and I crawled out of what was left of
Baldy Bird and realized that we were intact physically,
the comprehension came of how terrible it could have
been if one or the other of us had been seriously injured.
Just having to sit there and watch the other dying or
anyone for that matter, would have been unbearable.
We were humbled once again.

Perhaps that has nothing to do with it though.
Some say that when it is your time to go – you go! A
doctor friend once told me that in his experience, the
difference between life and death was often nothing
more than a scratch. And that for sure had been the
case here! At other times in my life too, I was
certainly aware that it must not have been my time "to
go" but I was not making that a part of my belief
system just yet. Still, by all practical purposes, I should
have been dead. It was right after the year we
experimented and dropped out of the rat race to that
tiny farm in Wisconsin.

*　*　*　*　*

I was anxious to fly once again after being unemployed for that winter, and although I thoroughly enjoyed the experience of being jobless, I figured it was time to get on somebody's payroll once more, even if it was just for the summer. Little did I know that the road I would be going down would be jobless from then on.

"Sure..I can git ya'll back in a helicopter again." It was Emery's Okie drawl at the other end of the line. "But ya'll have to be here in person to do it."

I'd finally reached him in Fairbanks. The big oil discovery on Alaska's North Slope was making headlines daily. I had been part of all that the previous summer and now would get a chance to return. I was to fly into Anchorage and find Vern Clamp who would line me out on the flying job. Emery would talk to him in the meanwhile but would be back on the Slope before I could get there.

Alaska's controversial pipe line project had been under severe cross-fire from the environmentalists since its inception, and sure enough—the day I rolled into Anchorage to go to work, they got it closed down completely. This was in June, 1970.

"There's nothing I can do." Vern said. "No one expected this." I'd known Vern from before when he was the camp chief at Kad River and we had gotten to be good friends.

"Listen," he said sympathetically, "Why don't you come stay with us for awhile? We're going up to Gulkana this weekend to do some king salmon fishing. You'll really enjoy it."

Vern had seven kids—all at home! When I hesitated, he persisted and with a twinkle said: "Heavens, we probably won't even notice you are there."

I couldn't resist. The Clamps were a marvelous family together. Everyone helped the other — the oldest down to the youngest — and they all adored Vern. The day we went fishing, I had misplaced my heavy-duty spinning reel, so missed out on the kings, but Vern got two and the kids had a ball romping about on that gravel bar all day, and roasting hot dogs on the campfire.

On the way home, with most of the kids sleeping in the back of the station wagon, Vern and I had a chance to talk about my options. He knew I was broke and had come to Alaska on a one-way ticket. I would need some kind of a job just to get back to Wisconsin, not counting accumulating a bit of a nest egg to make it through another winter.

"Why don't you try commercial salmon fishing?" Vern finally asked. "My neighbor does it every year and makes a bundle."

"How do you do that?" My ears perking up at the fishing part.

"I don't know, but we can go talk to him first thing tomorrow."

Sleep was long in coming that night. Getting paid to fish! I could hardly believe it. The thought kept going around and around in my head. And a "bundle" besides. I was excited but I knew something primordial had been awakened deep inside me.

Vern's neighbor had already gone to the fishing grounds. "Just left yesterday," his wife said. "Won't see him until August now."

The Alaska Department of Fish and Game office secretary told me, "If I were just starting out, I'd head to Bristol Bay. They are expecting the largest run of salmon in history out there this year. In fact, that's why there's nobody in this office. They are all out there."

Well, there are no roads to Bristol Bay and I certainly couldn't afford to fly "out there" as they say, so I did some re-thinking and decided to hitch-hike the two hundred miles to Homer, hoping to get on a boat in Prince William Sound. Even if it weren't the number one place in Alaska to fish that year — I needed a job.

All the crews were busy doing last-minute preparations when I finally arrived at the "end of the road," literally, in Homer. I had gotten there too late, it seemed, but walking the long docks, I found myself completely enthralled by the diversity of the boats in this little harbor town. Every model since Columbus had somehow found its way to the end of the road as well. Boxes of food and cases of soda, beer,and milk were being put aboard. Nets, too. Some going on, others coming off. Paint brushes were flying and you could tell there was an urgency about all this. The salmon were coming and each year these tiny boats went out to intercept them. It would be a frantic few weeks and then it would be all over for another year. The crabbers and shrimpers worked much longer, of course, but they were the minority here.

Then a guy stopped me and said: "Hey, aren't you the fellow we passed on the way down here from Portage the other day when you were hitch-hiking?"

"Yeah, maybe I was," I replied, barely recognizing him. They had been towing a large boat with his pickup and it was the only ride offer I'd refused on my two-day trip down here. It had been raining at the time and about 40 degrees. They only had room in the back because there were already four crowded into the cab as it was. I had told them that I didn't think I would survive back there because I didn't have much of a raincoat with me.

Now he stuck his big hand out, his wide grin matching the size of his frame. "I'm Mel Sanders. You looking for a job?"

"Yes." I almost blurted.

"Well, it's not exactly a job, but it might get you one," he went on enthusiastically. "We're taking that bow picker you saw us towing over to Bristol Bay and could use another hand along the way. Got any experience on boats?"

"Canoes," I said, realizing when the word was out that my credentials were rather limited for this ocean stuff. "Pretty fair mechanically, though," I quickly added, trying to salvage something from the first opportunity to come my way.

"We're leaving on this afternoon's tide right over at the boat ramp." He was pointing as he spoke. "Got my two daughters along and my son-in-law fresh out of the Navy, but I'd feel better if we had another hand along. Got a fishing crew all lined up in the Bay, but once we're there, I'll introduce you around. You should find something."

His positiveness was the most refreshing thing I'd heard in this fishing business since Vern first mentioned it.

Bristol Bay, I knew, was two hundred miles further west as the seagulls go — by sea, well over a thousand because you had to go out to False Pass and back again, which was the first connecting link through the Aleutian Chain which separated the North Pacific and the Bering Sea. Going over the portage at Williamsport was the other possibility, if your boat was small enough to fit through the overhead bridge structure at Pile Bay. Still, the trip would be something like two hundred and fifty miles, and it was not to be underestimated. There were maybe seventy-five miles of open ocean between Homer and Williamsport. And Cook Inlet, I'd been told, could get downright testy if a "SouWester" blew up. The portage was over sixteen miles of winding narrow gravel road across a tight fitting suspension bridge. The boat was balanced on top of a flat-bed truck, which then dumped you unceremoniously into Lake Iliamna. Its eighty-mile length makes it Alaska's largest freshwater lake. Wind there could be a problem, too, and there were rocks to worry about as well. After all that, there was still the seventy-five miles or more of the Kvichak River which dumped out of Iliamna to negotiate before you actually arrived in Naknek, the tiny fishing village on the northeast tip of Bristol Bay where the big salmon run was expected. No...it was not a trip to be taken lightly.

But the blue sky and the snowy topped mountains surrounding Homer, coupled with the bluish-green, gently rolling swells of the Pacific lulled me into believing this fishing thing was going to be a summer's dream. My peacefulness was short-lived.

"Where are we headed?" I casually asked no one in particular not long after we had gotten under way.

The "Navy boy" was driving so he spoke up. "Just south of that volcano on the horizon. It's Mt. Iliamna and it's ten thousand feet high."

"Where's the compass?" I asked as nonchalantly as possible as I glanced around the cabin, trying to keep my mind occupied and not wanting to let on to anyone that the sea swells were getting to my midwestern equilibrium.

"Oh we didn't get it unpacked yet." said the Navy captain. "Just finished building this thing a couple of days ago." Mel was napping and the Navy kid was using the opportunity to its fullest.

"Naval architect, too!" I thought. His continuous monologue of his Navy feats were not sitting well with the nauseousness that was beginning to displace the primordial feelings I had in my bones a few days prior.

I glanced at the puffy cummies to the south and was grateful for the weather. I knew full well that even in a canoe, a compass was a must if the sky decided to dump on you. Rooting around, I eventually found the compass box and set it unopened near the instrument panel where it would be handy just in case.

Slowly, the drone of the engine and the gentle swells and warm afternoon sun streaming through the port windows lulled me into a napping mood. Mel was up and the Navy was down so it was quiet at last. At the first cough the new Volvo inboard/outboard made, I was on my feet. Then it was silent. The ocean stretching endlessly on all sides was slick calm and the boat lazily rode up and down on the swells. I wondered if this was the calm before the storm I'd always heard about?

"You know anything about engines, Ted?" Mel asked, his voice hushed as though he were about to enter a mortuary. Mr. Navy himself was standing right there and he's asking me? I was beginning to understand a lot of things about this trip. For sure, they didn't tell me everything before I signed on.

"You got a book on this thing?"

"Only the owner's manual," which Mel was digging out of the food box while he spoke. I marveled at the organization once more but only to myself.

"There were only three things that can be wrong with any car when it quits. It's either not getting fuel, not getting any spark, or it's broken." My dad's words were coming back to me, but I wondered if they applied to boats in the middle of the ocean.

My queasiness returned. Engine compartments that you have to stand on your head to reach were not my idea of a work shop. There was plenty of gas so I started tracing wires and found a fuse panel with a twenty amp fuse burned out. Miraculously, Mel found some spares and we were under way once again. The tension release was apparent. Even the Navy, I noticed, had now asked me a question or two, but I couldn't revel in the spotlight for long. Remaining aloof while bending over the rail with seasickness is nearly impossible.

"Williamsport should be right up ahead." Mel shouted from the bow. He had a chart in his hand studying the shore line and motioned the Navy to turn her to port. An hour later, still cruising south, Mel came inside. "Got to be here somewhere."

I sure hoped so. I was starving now. "Got anything to eat on here?" I asked in a tone that was now not quite so subservient as when the trip started.

"There's a case of babyfood under that counter there," Mel said pointing but not taking his eyes off the shoreline.

Babyfood (peaches and pears) was not exactly what I had in mind but it went down well on a freshly empty stomach.

"That has got to be the place!" Mel said again as he took over the wheel and turned back to the north, heading for the small opening in the cliffs we'd been following for some time now. I was relieved that he was doing the driving because the rugged walls almost swallowed our tiny boat as we turned to the left and made our way deeper into the darkening fiord. Giant boulders, with their tell-tale white foam rings, were menacingly close as we slid by. Mel backed off on the throttle even more.

About a mile up the shoreline we could just barely make out the outline of a boat moored to a dock. We had arrived at Williamsport! The first leg of our journey lay behind us.

The tide, however, had already been to Williamsport and left again before we arrived. About a half mile from the dock, we slid to a halt on the mud bottom. Might just as well have been twenty miles because we were stranded for six hours where we were. It was definitely now time to eat.

"You mean the only food you actually have on board is a case of babyfood?" I couldn't believe it.

"Figured we better get going while the weather was good!" Mel answered, polishing off his second jar and starting on a third. All peaches, I noted.

With five of us, I wondered how long the case would last but was grateful that someone had grabbed fruit off the shelf, and not carrots or split peas in his haste.

Later when I awoke, we were tied against the other boat at the dock. The grey morning light was beginning to filter in over the towering peaks to the east. I headed for the shore constipated as heck. There was no bathroom on board, and I certainly was not yet accustomed to using a bucket with females so close and practically zero privacy on board.

In my daypack along with my camera and binoculars, I found some dried fruit. At least I could chew on that. But my stomach felt funny. "Probably left over from my seasickness," I thought, and let it go.

We were second in line to go over the portage and Mel really had to do some fast talking to get Carl Williams to take two boats over in one tide. The portage was really a state-maintained gravel road. The fact that

Williams also had the state contract to maintain the road of which he was the principal user seemed incomprehensible to someone like myself, but no one else seemed to even question it. The technique normally was to back his big eighteen-wheeler flatbed down into the salt water and let you float into place on the chocks. With Mel's persuasiveness and a winch they devised, Carl agreed to return for a second trip on this tide. It was tricky but they finally managed to slide the bow picker into place in the rapidly receding waters; still, it was late afternoon before we were finally dumped into Lake Iliamna — too late to travel on the lake. Thank God for that because Mrs. Williams invited us for supper.

My first meal in a real wilderness home! Her kitchen was as modern as any, except for the old wood stove beside her gas range. The big pot of caribou stew and homemade bread she served was the most welcome thing I'd seen or smelled in 48 hours. It was all I could do not to take the fourth serving she offered almost insistently. "Must be from the midwest somewhere," I thought, having experienced the same thing with all my wife's relatives in Wisconsin.

After the meal, there was time to learn some more about this place and Pile Bay and the portage road that led out to civilization. The grizzly bear rug on the wall next to Carl's chair had been a "real bear" under the front steps one morning when their youngest had stepped outside. The kids were all grown and gone from home now, but Carl fondled the rug as though it had all happened yesterday.

Our plan was to leave at first light to take advantage of the typically calm mornings on the lake. The eighty miles would take us about five to five and a half hours, Mel figured. Sleeping on a full belly sure felt better than on a jar of strained peaches. Still, 3 a.m. came way too soon.

Lake Iliamna just may be one of the most picturesque spots in Alaska. Scattered spruce-covered islands dot its rocky southeast shoreline, which is where we planned to travel as there was little protection to the north in case the wind blew up. Looking down into the sparkling water was disturbing, however, because the huge rocks were visible, and it was hard to tell how deep they were. I'd already had enough excitement without a hole being punched into the bottom of the boat. The Navy was back in charge once again, obviously having been re-promoted after last night's great meal and the sleep we all needed. The engine problem was now long forgotten by everyone.

Out on the front deck, I was enjoying the scenery against the glassy water. Sea gulls were on this inland sea and bald eagles, too. Their screeching filled the dawn above the now steady drone of the Volvo.

Iliamna, I knew, had one of the world's two fresh water seal herds, the other being in Russia. It was also the home of the largest run of salmon in the world. The warm, good feeling I'd had in my bones earlier was coming back once more as I sat there with the breeze of our movement blowing in my face. I was about to be part of this commercial fishing thing — one way or another.

But things have a way of going their own direction at times which is what happened when the Navy headed off the big lake and into the mouth of the Kvichak River at full steam! The rock kicked the stern with such a jolt that we were all on our feet instantly.

"Straighten her out and slow down!" I yelled back from the bow, more angry at having the tranquility gone than the Navy's driving. Again I'd been lulled into feeling safe on a boat, but it wasn't working out that way.

We were turning to the left (port I was to learn eventually) far too fast for comfort. The Navy idled it back, but the turn continued and we were about to crash into the river bank.

"Shut it off! Shut it off!" I yelled again, running back to the wheel house. Mel had grabbed the wheel but nothing seemed to work. The rudder had somehow sheared.

We got a line to the willows on the shore and assessed the damage. "Can you fix it, Ted?" Mel asked, the Navy seemingly having been granted a leave of absence once again.

"I don't know. Have you got some wire?" And astonishingly enough, he did. The splice wouldn't take any rocks but at least we were soon on our way once more.

The river was fun. The transparent water from Iliamna still predominated the upper reaches of what's been termed the finest sports fishing river left on the earth. Fast moving, with sweeping, gravel strewn curves, it was hard sometimes to keep the boat moving faster than the current to maintain control.

Mel kept saying, "Which channel, Ted?" as if I'd been down there a dozen times. The river had broken up into a wide delta with a series of channels, some dangerously shallow .

"Which way now?"

"Take the one to the right and head straight for the V," I said, pointing to the spot. My canoeing experience was obviously not so meager a qualification after all. I knew the problems inherent with downstream travel, because if you got hung up on a rock, the water pressure

behind you compounded the problem. It was bad enough getting off in a canoe. In this tub, it would be next to impossible.

But it happened. There just wasn't enough water in one of the channels I had chosen, and we became grounded — fortunately, on gravel and not impaled on a rock as I feared. We pushed with the pike poles and tried reverse, but it wasn't enough.

"We'll have to get in the water and push it off," I finally conceded.

Mel clung to the wheel while glancing toward the Navy, whose eyes were now studying the deck, his shoulders sagging badly. A bathtub full of ice cubes could not have prepared us for what followed. And even fully clothed to conserve some heat, it was terrible. At first only knee-deep, we heaved with everything we had. The Navy's contribution was his 140 pounds against my nearly 200, and together it was all we could do to make a dint with Mel roaring it in reverse. But slowly, the bow picker inched its way backwards into deeper water. Our feet dug into the gravel and the water temperature sent pains into our groins, but eventually the old tub floated free. We were soaked well above our waists when we finally clambered aboard, peeling off our clothes and getting into something dry.

By late afternoon, we'd been drenched a half dozen times by taking the wrong channel, but the five miles of delta now was behind us. Up ahead we could see the *Quincy*, which had crossed the portage just before us. It had anchored and its crew was waving us over.

The fried rainbows and grayling and the canned corn and bread rivaled Mrs. Williams' caribou stew. But being starved does wonders like that. I noticed that the babyfood peach deserts went untouched except for Mel downing a few.

It really felt good to rest and get acquainted with these three new guys. They too were going to Bristol Bay for the first time, but unlike our aluminum bow picker, they were bringing an old wooden Bryant which had the cabin forward and the work area in the stern, the reverse of ours. It had undergone a lot of recent repairs, judging from the unpainted boards I saw spliced in here and there. Unfortunately, they missed a few things, as the main shaft had snapped which was why we had caught up to them now. They would need a new one before they could continue.

We deliberated about towing them with us the next day, but they all finally agreed that it would be best to leave the *Quincy* here with one of the guys to watch it while the other two joined us for the last leg of the trip. Naknek was still more than a day away, meaning we would be spending a night at Nakeen, an abandoned cannery along the way, where Mel had evidently arranged for us to stop over. Anyway, we would now have seven on board.

In the morning everyone made for the beach for a final brush stop. When I had awakened, I was feeling a bit nauseous with my bowels rumbling and was especially glad to get to the shore.

"Probably some kind of a reaction to the cold water of yesterday," I reasoned with myself.

The river was easier now. The ocean tides were evident and the Navy had a couple more pairs of eyes helping him navigate the increasingly muddy water. I was grateful for the chance to be able to stay in my bunk down in one of the fish holds. It felt better not to have to move for some reason, and I slept off and on most of the day.

Scuffling about and shouting on the deck, followed by a crunching of aluminum against something, brought me to my feet from a sound sleep. The Navy had landed once again.

My first impressions of Nakeen came from looking straight up a muddy, algae-coated wooden ladder that seemed to go up into the ozone.

"The tide's out, so bring your sleeping bag unless you want to climb this thing twice," Mel said over his shoulder as he started the climb.

Bob, from the *Quincy*, had waited for me.

By now my stomach was not just upset, it physically hurt if I touched it the wrong way. I knew the climb was going to be tough.

"I'll bring your stuff, Ted. You just get up the ladder." Bob must have sensed something even I didn't yet.

My impressions of Nakeen changed little from the surface. Wooden walkways went everywhere, and buildings of all sizes and descriptions towered along the river bank and back into the tundra. The afternoon sun, which was evening actually, hung low over the dark clouds in the west. I half expected a thunderbolt to crash and the shutters to start banging. Had it been raining, the place would have been right out of a Hitchcock movie.

For me, climbing the long steps up to a dusty, bunk-filled room in what they called the men's bunk house was painful. Mel and the girls stayed with the watchman and, I assume, ate there as well. I was grateful for the bed but remembered wiping my arm across the filthy window just in time to see the sun disappear below the distant tundra. I felt strange but didn't know why.

Darkness comes slowly in June. Sleep did, too. Morning light found me out on the boardwalks, still trying to figure out what was wrong. Later, when I tried some of the oatmeal we were all offered for breakfast, I knew it was coming back up and had to leave the kitchen in a hurry.

It was good to be underway once again, away from the dust and smelling the salty air. The seacoast was definitely getting closer. Unfortunately, we did not.

Even by now, this Pennsylvania boy had figured out something about tides: Six hours to come in and six hours to go out, give or take a little each day. In our case, we had arrived at the old cannery after 10 p.m. looking up a ladder to nowhere, which meant the tide was out or nearly so. It would have been a simple matter to leave six hours later to catch the high tide at 4 a.m., except we had left at 8.

Two hours later, we were fighting shallow, muddy water with no idea of where the channels went. The river had long since given up its pristine crystalness to silt and mud of the big flats in which we now found ourselves mired.

"That's OK, we can go on in the skiff and get your part ordered and our new rudder linkage and get back here on the next tide." It was Mel—always full of enthusiasm and a way out.

I could hear them unloading the skiff and Mel and the *Quincy* crew piling aboard, bidding their festive farewells to the girls while the Navy was to watch over things. I was still in my fish hold bunk when I heard them pulling away and then returning.

"We better take Ted along," I could hear Bob saying to the Navy and the girls above. "He's pretty sick."

I crawled out of my nest, hurting too much to argue. It was all I could do to move.

"Better wrap him in a sleeping bag."

The rest of the trip gets a little fuzzy for me, but I'm sure that single move saved my life. Although they tried their darnedest to do me in along the way! I remember huddling down below the gunwales and seeing the waves above my head but not caring. When we ran out of gas along the way, Mel got as close to the shore as possible and then jumped into the water and traipsed into the brush with the gas can. It wasn't long before he was back, having talked an Eskimo out of a gallon. Good old Mel.

We ran out of gas a second time, but by then Naknek was just down the beach.

"Come on, Ted, we can walk from here." And arms were under mine on each side as we started down the gravel beach, the *Quincy* crew helping me while Mel led the way into town. Climbing up the last bank was terrible but as soon as we did, the two *Quincy* guys looked around to get their bearings and said: "The health nurse is up there somewhere," pointing to another hill which made the last one seem easy. And with that they disappeared into the *Red Dog Saloon*, leaving me on the street. I never saw or heard from them again.

When I knocked on the door of the Borough Health Office, tears were streaming down the cheeks of a grown man. "You're in trouble, aren't you?" she said, grabbing her coat. "Come on, let's get you into my car and over to the doctor!"

The doctor took a look at me, asking the usual questions; when he pressed in on my stomach and then quickly took his hand away—I yelled. "You've got appendicitis, boy! You're going to the hospital. Can't do nothing for you here."

The chartered flight had to be gassed up and serviced, and it seemed everyone who came by the waiting room knew the test for appendicitis.

"Yep, you've got it," they said. I gasped as I flinched but muffled my yell once more. I would have liked to have kicked every one of them in the shins if I could have managed it. Yet they were all sympathetic.

When I arrived in Dillingham, the ambulance was waiting. With no money, in borrowed clothes and no underwear, (since it was impossible to dry anything the past few days) I'm sure I was a sorry sight. I was operated on that night, but not before the Public Health Intern summoned Doctor Libby off his fishing boat to come and assist. This would be the intern's first appendectomy and he wanted someone there in case he got into trouble.

All I remember was seeing the white gowns and people all around me. But my troubles were far from over.

I woke up in a grey morgue-like room. The wall and floor tiles were cracked; the faded window shades were partially drawn and light streamed in from the fluorescent hall lights. A chubby middle-aged nurse was tugging on my arm.

"Come on, come on. It's time to get up and walk." Her indifference to my pain was more than obvious.

"Oh, don't worry, your insides are not going to fall out on the floor!" She must have gone to the same school as the cannery doctor who first examined me.

Later, the intern visited. "Well, we can expect another appendectomy any time now. A fourteen-year-old girl came in this morning while you were still out. Everything happens in three's around here it seems." He rambled on. "You should be out of here in a week or so. I think we got you cleaned out OK. Your appendix burst when we opened you up. Good thing you got here when you did."

I made a call to Penny in Wisconsin. She was frantic, but there was nothing she could do. The doctor had ordered me not to fish when I got out. Pulling on the nets could pull my side open. I would do what I could do to get us some money to make it through the winter and promised to call her when I knew something definite.

Eventually I was released, and the realities of the real world came crashing down almost immediately. Since I had arrived in no underwear, had no money and had had to sign my life away for the charter flight, I would be on my own getting back to Naknek. A commercial flight left every day at noon, and I was headed out the door without a dime in my pocket when one of the nurses I had gotten to know came to say goodbye and shake my hand. In it, she placed the fare.

"Not a word," she whispered as she put a finger to her lips. "I'd lose my job."

My eyes were still tearing as I sat on the flight back to Mel and the bow picker. They were headquartered at the Nelbro cannery. It didn't take as long to find them as I expected, and there I found my belongings stuffed under a shed as well.

It was still too soon to get a cannery job with my side the way it was. My money supply was practically nil after I sent the airplane fare back to the nurse. The charter would have to wait a while longer on theirs. Mel questioned me at one point as to whether the cold water and the pushing had caused all this. I wondered if he was more concerned with his liability than my welfare, but only replied that it was too bad I hadn't purchased my commercial fishing license before going into the hospital because Fisherman's Fund would have picked up the tab. As it was, I would get the whole thing: A year off, a one-way ticket north, and now a $3000 hospital bill, and it wasn't over yet.

There was no place to sleep in Naknek unless you were on a boat, or working at a cannery, or could afford a room at the one overcrowded inn. It was better for me to camp out, so I made a tent of sorts from some plastic I scrounged and set about recuperating on the bank of the river just out of town. Patty, one of Mel's daughters, sneaked me into the cannery mess hall from time to time having me pose as a crew member on their boat, but I felt uncomfortable doing that.

I spent my days walking the cliffs overlooking the Naknek River, and watched with fascination the boats below. Fishing was closed right now. The canneries were glutted. I had come so close.

Later, I was sitting on a high overlook wondering how I was going to feed myself on a regular basis when I noticed a bit of paper tangled deep in the grass between my legs. It turned out to be a small raisin box dropped by some passerby. I dug it out and could hardly believe my good luck when I found it was unopened. Looking around, I found a second buried near the first—also untouched. I couldn't remember a meal tasting so sweet, so rich, or so fulfilling.

Afterward, I was down on the beach and saw where a truck had dumped a whole load of spoiled salmon. "Salmon. I could eat salmon!" If they can waste this much, surely I would be able to find one to eat. But how to cook it? My camp was more sparse than most. Walking still further along the beach and more or less lost in my thoughts and listening to the ruckus the gulls were making, I practically bumbled into an old fire grate. My needs were met.

A lump was developing on my side where they operated, and my belt was putting a dent in it which I noticed when I crawled into my sleeping bag in the still light night. "Swelling from the healing process," I reasoned and went to sleep.

I was wandering along the paths between the cannery buildings at mid-morning when a Cushman scooter stopped in front of me. "You looking for a job?" It was the cannery superintendent. I told him of my plight, but he said he couldn't take a chance on my side splitting open and drove off behind me. Then I heard the brakes screech.

"Come on!" he yelled. "I'll find you something." I crawled in behind him, and we were off at once.

"You got any education, Ted?" he asked as he turned corner after corner faster than my side felt comfortable.

"I've got a Bachelor of Science degree from Penn State."

"Oh, yeah? I'm from back that way myself." We were friends instantly.

My job was to stamp the code numbers on the salmon cases as they came off the assembly line. Other guys stacked the boxes onto pallets for shipping. I was grateful at noon when I could eat fully relaxed, since I had not been smuggled in under false pretenses. The 3 p.m. coffee break was just as welcome. Later, when we returned to the assembly line, Mother Nature called on me, so I left the line to take care of things and was appalled at the puss I found running down my right thigh from the dint my belt had made in the lump on my side. I was actually split open.

The superintendent could not believe his ears and slapped his forehead in disbelief. He summoned a young fellow to drive me up to the doctor's office in his pick-up. It was the same doc who had diagnosed my appendicitis in the first place and when he spoke, I understood why he was not in some prosperous practice elsewhere.

"You've got a mess here, boy," he said as he squeezed gobs of the oozing puss from my side with gauze pads. "Don't know if you're going to make it this time."

The young fellow who brought me here turned white and sagged against the door. The anger that was within me took me by surprise. My senses could not believe my ears. I never expected to die lying down nor wanted to, but this was an insult to something deep inside me.

There were some good things though. Now the cannery had to send me back to Dillingham in their plane and I got to take all my belongings with me. And the intern greeted me with a bit more compassion than the quack I had just left.

"We'll have to open you back up to let this drain. You can be thankful that it broke outward and not inside. A massive infection like this would be impossible to quench otherwise."

There **was** hope! I felt the life within me surge once again and the optimism I'd always known return almost at once. I would be in the hospital several more weeks. My commercial fishing venture was all but finished...but not quite.

Jim Berry came into the hospital for a short stay with some kind of a stomach disorder. He was from Michigan, our neighboring state, and was learning to operate a boat over at Queen Fisheries which he would be running the following year. Would I like to be his deck hand?

"YOU BET I WOULD!"

Somehow, Penny scraped up enough money to get me home and was waiting for me at the airport in

Minneapolis. She had stayed with Murf and his wife Marilyn, an old friend and fellow Penn Stater. Murf offered me some temporary work planting trees with his big tree spade so I could get out from under my hospital bills as soon as I felt up to it.

Penny applied for and got the only job to come open in our little country school since it was built, and we made it through another winter in her Aunt Sylvia's little red farmhouse.

There was some sad news, though. Wally Adams, a fellow who used to sell me turfgrass seed when I was on the golf course, had been rushed into a hospital in Minneapolis/Saint Paul with appendicitis at the same time I was finding my way through the delta on the Kvichak with a pain in my side. He died on the operating table.

chapter 6

It is not yet noon here on the tundra. We have to count the days now by remembering special things we have done. It is interesting to see how much we have settled into our new lifestyle since the crash. Our fourth day we decide.

The day is bright and cheery and the breeze just enough to keep the bugs tolerable. We find ourselves at the river early, a change from our routine. The tart breakfast blueberries which went down rather well the first few days when we still had some bread to eat with them and thought we were leaving the next day, now seem too harsh. Hot fish is on our minds...if we can catch one.

Yesterday, we were not so lucky and lost many of the lures I had in the survival gear to the underwater snags that blocked our fishing hole. This is the third major hole we have explored. All have spawned-out king salmon holding on their nearby nests, but neither of us can bear to kill them.

Often, on my own boat, I've turned especially energetic fish back overboard. Just to see their exuberance made me feel good somehow. No, these spawners were safe as far as we were concerned.

Whit and I both fish commercially. He works as a partner on the *Herbert Cecil*, owned by his best friend Frank; and I work for myself on the *Tin Can*. I say work because it is not a job by our definition. Jobs for Whitney and me were those things that keep a person penned up 9 to 5 wishing they were somewhere else. Fishing was something completely different. Once in your blood, it is much like flying or possibly drugs. Another fix is all you crave.

* * * * *

I never set out to become a commercial fisherman. I always thought of myself as a glorified farmer of sorts. Boats, though, were another matter.

My dad had me out on Lake Erie on a party boat fishing for blue pike before I was out of grade school, and I'd be so sea sick I couldn't feel the fish biting on my line. I can also remember playing in our flat bottom river boat on French Creek as a child; paddling it upstream as far as the rope that was tied to shore would let me go and then having the current swing me around in a gentle arc for the short free ride I'd get for my efforts. When the line snapped once and I went sailing downstream, my panicked screams brought my dad and his friend down off the cabin roof they were shingling. His friend, running full bore down the bank and into the now waist-deep water, managed to grab the boat before it got swept into the fast water under the bridge and eventually to the rapids below.

I was terrified, but my dad would not let me get out of the boat. He insisted I keep paddling and playing as I had been. "It was just a weak knot," he reassured me. I did not always realize my father's wiseness, but I did what he said — that time. Boats, of all descriptions, I have loved from that time forth.

Tar Baby was the first craft I ever built, and despite its very appropriate christening, it did get me into some pretty hot bass fishing in the swamp near our home. Later, I got an open kayak and although it was easier to get around with, I ripped a five-foot gaping hole in its bottom once on a snag and never trusted it in the swamp after that. So I painted it a flamboyant green with white stripes and used it to play with on open water instead.

I was married already when I managed to bring home my first true love — a canoe — an *Old Town* no less. It happened to be my wife's birthday and the fact that it was her dad who found it for me made little impression when I got back too late for us to go out for her celebration dinner. The canoe, nearly fifty years old then, has survived the test of time and I still have and use it.

Although canoes have always been number one on my list, whenever I got near a marina, I drooled over the big boats. There were so many different types and styles, and I always wondered about the people who operated them. The fact that they actually got paid for being on a boat was incomprehensible to someone who thought he was a farmer.

And so when Vern Clamp let me off at the dock in Anchorage a year before, apologizing because that was all he knew about salmon fishing, I had come a long way. Meeting Jim in the hospital in Dillingham when I had appendicitis and having him ask me to be his deck hand for the following season was a dream come true, I thought. I should have taken better stock of my boating experience up to then because I was about to learn some hard lessons.

Jim had said in his letter to fly into Dillingham and take a Cub over to Queen Fisheries. He would be there by mid-June. I got there on Father's Day and we launched the *Pollyanna* — a bow picker sort of a thing with an outhouse-sized cabin perched on its stern. It even had the proverbial half-moon window built into the door, but looking back, that was all it had in the way of class. A compass and a radio and three ragged nets were all we had to complete our outfit, but we thought we were "top-of-the-line" at the time. It turned out to be one of the worst ordeals of my life, so much so that I vowed that I would never work for another human being ever again. And for the next six years I didn't, but I paid for that stubbornness many times over.

It wasn't that Jim was such a bad guy. In fact, he was just the opposite — a very personable chap. But when we headed to sea that morning of the first opening, I began to have serious doubts about him. After driving through a misty fog with the sun trying its best to burn a hole down through the top for what seemed like hours to a novice like myself, Jim shut the engine down, walked out onto the deck, peered off into the mist in all directions, and announced with all the authority and assurance of a veteran sea captain (Jim had only the one previous summer's experience) — "Yep, this is the spot. We'll set the net here."

As the season progressed, my doubts about Jim grew. But he could sure keep that old Chevy engine running and he got us out of serious trouble more than once. Whenever it would stop, we usually were somewhere we shouldn't have been or needed to get away from as quickly as possible. Like being dragged over a sand bar or getting beached.

"Take the wheel," he'd say as he dashed out the door. The deck boards would be flying as he made his way down into the engine compartment. "Try her now!" he'd yell.

"Nothing."

"Now!" And bingo, it would start right off. I never learned what he did and didn't really care. Being rolled over a sand bar has a way of pumping more adrenalin into you than you can think sometime. It was enough just to get away from there. Oh, we caught fish that summer all right. There were lots to catch. But the grief never ended.

When he started smoking pot and being late for the openings, our relationship crumbled even more. Once when we backed over our nets and became entangled like the salmon we were catching, he was ready to quit for the season. I went over the side in my long johns with a rope tied to my waist and cut us free but was practically useless the rest of the day with my shivering, but at least we kept fishing. Another time, our rudder came apart at the dock just before an opening, and I had to find someone else to hold my feet while I again went underwater and repaired it, because my captain was no where to be found.

At sea once, he wanted to go visit another boat so we pulled up our nets and drove over to where they were. The next thing I knew, they were steaming towards town and I was alone on the ocean. I think that's when the last of our working relationship dissolved. At season's end we were barely speaking. We rode back to the lower 48 on the same airplane, and I was relieved to not have to sit in the same row with him. By Christmas though, I did manage to send him a pack of photos I'd taken during the summer that I knew he would enjoy. Jim never came back to Bristol Bay. It just was not in his blood to be on the sea.

But it was in mine. That feeling that is in your bones sometimes when you know something is right for you was there for me that first summer, even with all that happened. So before I left the cannery, I made some arrangements on my own for the following season. I would fish one of the company skiffs — alone.

And so I was free. For the first time in my life, I was out on my own. It was a fantastic feeling. I'd finally stumbled onto something where, if you kept your head about you and reasoned things out, and were willing to gamble just a bit beyond your reach, and could tough out the mistakes you made along the way, and were lucky at all, the satisfaction couldn't be surpassed. What you got was directly proportional to what you did — with some luck. I couldn't have asked for anything better to come into my life.

How I got through all the seasickness, I'll never know. I can remember bundling up in my woolen long johns and all of my heaviest clothing and then putting a rain suit on over that and freezing with the chills under a woolen blanket. I had a candle burning to keep me company as I huddled in the tiny cabin on the bow of my skiff, waiting for the next gagging spell. At the last possible moment, I'd dash out of my cubicle and lean over the gunwale, my insides churning with the little skiff's motion as the waves poured their wrath on all of us who had ventured out on such days. All I could do was crawl back into my little hole, now wringing wet with

Diane Hill

sweat from my vomiting, and wait for the cycle to repeat itself.

I did manage to always eat something right then, however. Fruit cocktail was one of my favorites. I had cans and cans of it stashed onboard for just such emergencies, and liked to tease the others about it.

"Fruit cocktail has two distinct advantages over any other seasick remedy on the market," I'd usually start out to anyone who showed any interest at all. "Number one, it tastes just as good coming up as it did going down." And if that didn't send them gagging, they would invariably ask for the second reason. "It's amazing stuff because when it comes back up, it hasn't even changed the way it looks."

Once though, it had been a particularly rough day and I'd gone through all my fruit cocktail and was now trying to keep down 7-Up and pilot crackers with about the same success as the fruit cocktail. Eventually, my throat and pipes to my stomach became so scratched from the hurriedly downed crackers that I gave up trying to eat anything at all. That was a mistake I will likely never make again, for the dry heaves with the green bile soon followed.

When the tide finally turned around, I knew it was time for me to get out of there. The waves had smoothed out somewhat, but when I tried to pull in the net, I found I was almost too weak to do so. But by watching the waves and waiting for the skiff to slide down the front side, I could get a single cork (about an arm's length) into the boat—fish, net and lead line as well. Usually, I would have been ecstatic at the number of fish coming aboard but not this time. The six hundred feet were endless, but when I was busy, I vomited less and eventually the end buoy came. I had a two-hour run against the southeast swells before I could get into calmer waters, but now I was so weak that I feared leaning over the side when my stomach revolted. Instead, I got down on my knees and put the steering lever and throttle of the fifty-horse Mercury under my armpit and hung on as best I could, keeping the bow quartering into the waves. I had quite a load on board, but if I could just hang on – I'd make it.

Soon though, I'd feel it coming. The wrenching in my stomach was not to be denied. Without taking my eyes off the distant horizon, so as not to lose my heading and possibly swamp myself by getting crosswise to the waves, I'd just gag, the green bile running down my chin and the front of my slickers. It didn't matter any more. I just had to get into the safety of Clark's Slough. The spray from the wind washing over me cleaned it off anyway.

When I made the quiet water in the slough, my skiffing friend Al was already there clearing his nets so I threw him a line and tied on alongside. "I've got to rest for a minute, Al," was about all I got out and with that, lay down where I was amidst the pile of net and slimy fish, my cheek coming to rest on the side of a red salmon, and was out.

My skiffing days lasted five years and physically I never felt better. It seemed there was nothing I couldn't do or at least would not try. Even though pulling in the nets by hand certainly could be hard work, it was satisfying, too. One moonlit night in particular, I'd just pulled in a boatload and was busy clearing the fish from the net when I realized how peaceful and quiet it was all around ne. I finally just stopped and went and lay down across the small deck on the bow and breathed it all in.

The smell of the sea air, the few gulls shrieking in the distance, the gentle sloshing of the sea against the skiff all came to me. Distant voices too came floating over the water from other boats with their lights flickering here and there. "Was I really getting paid to be here or is this some kind of a weird dream?" I wondered to myself. "Wouldn't it be something if I could get my dad up here to experience all this?"

And so I started weighing that feasibility. I knew he wouldn't think much of living in an open skiff in a 35 mph gale with horizontal rain. Maybe it was time I moved up to a "real boat?" I liked this "one foot in the mud type fishing" though. A big 32-foot power boat would represent a major change in attitude, and I wondered if I could muster that?

To me, fishing a skiff represented total freedom. "If I want to take off some summer and paddle my canoe across Canada instead of coming up here, I can do it," I told Al. He and I had often discussed moving up to a "real boat" and what we liked and didn't like about certain ones. One thing of which I was certain—I would have to have a boat that I could operate alone. I was never going to get myself in a situation where a helper was mandatory, and have a summer like my first one. Also, the boat I would get would have to be able to sleep my 6'4" Dad.

Baldy was operated by Jon Coffeen and I'd often seen him out fishing alone, at least part of the season. I liked its beautiful three-tone green and white paint scheme and the wide swept flare of its bow and the flying bridge which Jon used extensively when fishing by himself. Its yellow cedar hull was one of the best of the wooden boats in the bay. Often, I'd sit up on the dock at the cannery and look down over the different vessels, watching their owners and crew going about their various routines. I imagined myself in each of their places, but it was only on *Baldy* where I really fit.

One day at coffee break, I heard Jon and his brother talking about the new boat design they hoped to bring up to the bay someday—possibly even next summer. If they did, could I have the first chance at buying *Baldy*? I gave them $20.00 when I left to make the phone call and couldn't wait to get home that fall to let my dad know about my decision. It was the first year I'd really made any money with my skiff and the first time I'd ever seen a $10,000 check, let alone one made out to me.

En route to Wisconsin, I was notified that my dad had dropped dead of a heart attack at his home in Pennsylvania. I was barely able to make the funeral in time. The ten grand had little joy in it by then. I was the last surviving member of my family of four. Certainly there is no such thing in life as security. More determined than ever, I would go after whatever was left for me of my remaining days on this earth. A poster that caught my eye soon afterward said: *Don't wait for your ship to come in. Swim out after it!* And so I did.

Baldy was to become mine, with Northern State Bank as co-owner. It was the first time in my life that I had gone into debt. Boat ownership suddenly shifted my attitude towards fishing, though. Oh, I was still determined to do it alone—especially that first year. Something inside me insisted on completing the circle of being let off at the dock in Anchorage and walking back into the bank with the cash in my hand to pay off the loan. And when I did just that, I plopped a 38 pound king salmon down along with the money as sort of a token of my appreciation for trusting me. The loan officer and I made the front page of the local newspaper with that one, and he made vice president of the bank shortly afterward. We became good friends, and he has helped me many times since with my financial dealings.

But there was something else. Something much more subtle to this fishing than making money. Part of it was my having been accepted and on a par, into a world that only six years before, I couldn't even comprehend. These guys, who I knew to be fiercely independent, sometimes belligerent, ever resourceful, and usually suspicious of greenhorns, had accepted me into their fold. Yes, I'd come a long way from that helicopter job I lost in Anchorage; but it didn't matter. Here was something which I could really relate to. The rewards I had found in skiffing were to be found in power boats as well. Unfortunately, the responsibilities seemed to be much greater and my dreams of taking off for a summer and paddling my *Old Town* to Hudson Bay or across Canada have not yet been resolved. But getting into the fishing business and being able to really compete has been as exciting as anything I could have imagined in my life. My dad would have loved it.

Although I fished *Baldy* alone that first season in some of the toughest conditions in the bay, I have never fished entirely alone since. I've learned an awful lot about being a captain, too.

Some of what I learned had to do with poor Peter Maller, my first deck hand. As a newspaper reporter, he had come up from Wisconsin to do an article about my experiences and to lend a hand on the boat. He was not comfortable at sea and it was one of those summers where horizontal rain or thick fog was all too common. Once I found him putting on his life jacket just as I came down off the flying bridge after watching the sun set behind the mountains to the west over slick calm seas. It was one of the few perfect days all summer. We were planning to fish that night, along with about three hundred other boats.

"What are you doing?" I asked when I came into the wheel house.

"They just said on the radio that a big storm is coming—gail force winds! There are small craft warnings going up all the way down the chain."

I wonder how he survived and was still able to write the story.

Then there was Lee, my college roommate, who now had his PhD in entomology. He had come to Alaska to do some collecting in the summer of 1980 and did a stint with me on board *Tin Can*, the aluminum boat I have now that replaced *Baldy*. After four days, he asked to leave. Something in his genes couldn't survive the disorganization of fishing.

"What do you mean get the fish out?"

"So we can get the net back in the water and catch some more."

"And get it tangled again?" The thought was insane to him. The eleven thousand pounds we hauled in the first time we laid the net out was more fish than he could comprehend from his usual microscopic view of the world. He had none of the greediness inherent in all successful fishermen.

But greediness did not supersede loyalty. It was common to see one boat or several trying to rescue another who happened to get caught in shallow water or in trouble some other way. It was something you did without thinking because it could just as easily be you who was out there floundering.

Looking back, I really don't know what I would have done with my life had I not somehow bumbled into commercial fishing. Certainly, it opened avenues that would not have been feasible otherwise. And yet, it is possible that I could have flown airplanes.

chapter 7

There are no trees in this barren land and again, I am thankful for that. There are mountains, though, and they are all around us. We are on the lower slopes, looking out over a wide beautiful valley in the Yukon Delta National Wildlife Refuge.

A gentle flowing stream winds through the land below our camp, and scattered lakes can be seen in the distance. The tundra air is smooth and sweet. There are no human sounds. It is almost too picturesque to be real.

A flock of magpies swoops from nowhere into the nearby "pucker brush" which I believe to be dwarf birches. Opportunists, to be sure, they find no bones to pick here — this time. We still do not fully comprehend the reasons why. The remains of *Baldy Bird* lies on the tundra beside us. Death had looked us in the eye one moment and this scene was before us the next. Somehow, being humble wasn't enough.

As we lounged around or took walks to pass the time, my mind wandered back to the days of my youth.

Two things had always been apparent: Canoeing in Canada's wilderness; and coming to Alaska. Somehow, flying became part of my Alaskan dream. I had been told early-on that if I truly wanted to experience Alaska's wildness, I would have to learn to fly. More than that—I would have to figure some way to budget an airplane into my life. It was a long time coming, but so sure was I that I would own my own airplane someday that I stole the first aid kit out of the L-19 I flew in the army and kept it for fifteen years before I had a place to put it. And now, here it was lying beside us amidst the debris of the crash, still unopened. As I said, being humble didn't quite cover it.

But I had made a deal with *Baldy Bird* the day I got it and now did not have a gripe in the world. If ever it had to quit, no matter where, and I was still able to walk away, we were square. The slate was clean.

* * * * *

Everyone who flies can remember the day they knew it was what they wanted. I was in college and took an introductory ride in a little Cessna 150 for $5.00. It was a gimmick to get you hooked and it worked, but there was no money for lessons. Right after college the army caught up with me and I ended up in the infantry after being promised Officer Candidate School. The day they dropped the tear gas on us in a field maneuver and I looked up, still choking with the fumes burning my lungs and eyes, and saw those fellows in the L-19s having the time of their lives, I knew I had waited long enough. The army could teach me to fly. And so the army and I set about playing little games with each other, but eventually I was issued orders to go to Fort Rucker, Alabama, for my flight training. They came the day Kennedy was assassinated, but I would have remembered it anyway.

So all of a sudden, it was fifteen years later and I now had commercial ratings in both airplanes and helicopters and a first aid kit, but still nowhere to put it. I was driving past Merrill Field in Anchorage after fishing season and saw a sign. FOR SALE: 1956 "Super Cub Special" Only...$13,500.00! Well, it wouldn't hurt to look.

I'd had a deal with my wife for some time now, because owning an airplane had become a common subject around our house since I bought the boat for my commercial fishing.

"Ted, you can buy an airplane anytime you want, but I get to spend the same amount on anything I want, too."

It seemed fair all right when she said it. But on paper, it was not financially feasible.

"OK, half the amount of what you spend on an airplane."

Now we were talking! My search had really begun to get serious at that point. Through a fishing friend, I'd heard of a PA 12 out in Kansas that was in a barn and not flown anymore which I could get for $6,500 — still a lot of money but within the budget. This airplane even held three people — pilot in the front and two in the back, sitting side by side. We would all fit as a family! I am sure it was this line of reasoning that finally convinced her to succumb at all.

But here I was in Alaska — *Super Cub Country,* the guide's and bush pilot's work horse of the North. I had only stayed over after fishing season to learn something about buying airplanes before I went down to Kansas to look at the PA 12 in the barn.

"If you want a PA 12 to do what a Super Cub already does, why not just buy the Super Cub in the first place. It'll be a lot cheaper in the long run." It is dangerous to go up against a good salesman without all of your rebuttal guns fully loaded. Even more so after having gone for a test flight. He made sense and I knew it, but I didn't roll over just yet.

"Look, for the kind of flying I want to do, I'm going to need skis, winter wing covers and an engine muff. Wisconsin's winters can be just like living in Alaska sometimes. And, I never buy anything without sleeping on it first." There, I had said my piece and got myself out of there.

It is even more dangerous to confront a good salesman the next day because he caught me off guard. "All right, all right. If I get you the skis, find a set of wing covers and can dig up an engine muff somewhere, are you going to buy this airplane or not?"

Whew! I'd gotten myself deeper into a corner than I figured. He knew I had a big check in my pocket and had already assured me that I could cash it through his wife who worked at one of the local banks. I had my back literally up against the wall — his wall and I could feel the heat rising up through my shoulders and burning in my ears, my head spinning. I wanted an airplane so badly it was all I could think about. I'd already been in Anchorage for ten days and had looked at hundreds of airplanes and had talked with anyone who would listen. It all had pointed to just one thing — a Super Cub is what I really wanted.

The word just slipped out from between my lips almost in a whisper. The hot flashes went sailing off into space and my skin felt cool. I was almost floating. To this day, buying that airplane....even if I got killed in it tomorrow or yesterday, was the single best thing I have ever done for myself — ever. A dream had come true. I had an airplane of my very own but not just **any** airplane — a Super Cub.

There is really very little you actually know about airplanes, regardless of what you think you've learned, until you lay the money down on the table. Almost immediately there were some problems. The strobe light and the radio malfunctioned before I could move it off the lot. They were generous enough though to repair those things. Later, when I decided to change the tires to something more suitable for off-field landings, I found a cracked axle and, of course, it was now my privilage to pay for that. And ever since, the repair bills have never stopped coming, but neither has the magnificent pleasure of having and flying my own plane.

Fully loaded with all my summer fishing gear, along with the skis and winter covers, and what little was left of my once big check, I taxied for departure out of the Anchorage bowl area, which can be one of the busiest areas of the nation. I once read somewhere that over half of the privately-owned aircraft in the world are in Alaska – on Friday evenings, you may think they are all on Merrill Field! As my turn finally came, I hurriedly went through the pre-flight checks for the umpteenth time and started down Runway 15 on my way to Wisconsin nearly four thousand miles away, where I had not breathed a word to anyone of my purchase. But something didn't feel right and as the wheels lifted off the blacktop, I remembered. It had been nearly twelve years since I'd last flown a tail dragger. (An airplane of this type has its third wheel on the tail and is notorious for ground looping unless you stay pretty current in them.)

Kent Sandvik's grass strip, fifty miles out of Anchorage, was my first intended stop. Landing there was not to be underestimated, especially if the wind was coming down off the Knik Glacier, and it was. On my way past the Birchwood Airport, I made a few touch-and-go landings on their long blacktop runway. Shaky at best but controllable at least, I headed for Kent's strip. There the approach would be over the wires that ran along the road, and the corner of his new metal-roofed barn would be there to greet me, along with the irrigation pipes that lined the roadway through his field which they called the runway. With the tire tracks barely visible in the high grass, it was going to be marginal.

My instincts kept me well clear of the barn and the wires, but I couldn't get down in time to stop within the bounds of his field on my first approach, or the second, or the third. By now some of Kent's neighbors had joined him to watch the show, and I missed a couple more times. My only salvation would be to go over to Palmer and use their long paved runway before it got dark. But I was so close last time. Maybe one more try.

When the wheels brushed the grass, I chopped the power — down at last. It was an accident, I knew, and almost didn't admit it to Kent, but when I did he sure got on my case.

"You get in that thing tomorrow and run it up and down that field until it feels right again before you take off. You understand?" His orders were given out of love. Kent, although he didn't fly himself, knew about airplanes. Three of his pilot brothers had already died in them. It would have been easy for him to have been down on airplanes but he wasn't. When brother Mark was killed in the fiery crash of the Otter he was flying near Anchorage, Kent helped his son buy the J 5 from his widowed sister-in-law and encouraged him while he was learning to fly. It was the reason for the strip in the field. No, Kent knew the value of having an airplane in a land where few roads lead to anywhere.

He also had more faith in me than was warranted. His son and some friends were planning to fly up to a gold mine on Sunday in the Talkeetna Mountains to do some gold panning. I was invited to come along, and now four airplanes would be going in all. Kent would ride with me to show the way. But first I had to practice.

So early the next morning, under a brilliant blue and windless sky, with Pioneer Peak watching my every move, I unloaded the Cub and started its engine. It was surprising how responsive it was with no weight on board. Slowly at first, getting the feel of the rudder and brakes again, I was soon going full bore up and down the field—grass flying everywhere from the chop of the propeller. More than anything, I was itching for a bush landing.

I knew about the big sand bars up on the Knik River and finally, not being able to resist any longer, I let the Cub go airborne as I tore down the field for the dozenth time. The sand bars are really gravel that has been washed down from the glacier and many of them were marked with the tracks of airplanes as they landed and took off from various locations among the many channels of the river as it wound its way to the ocean not very distant. It was an excellent place for me to get started in this bush landing thing.

When the Cub rolled to a stop, I had to get out and experience what it was like to be actually in the wilds for the first time in my own airplane. I pulled the mixture and turned off the mags as I climbed out. The Big Silence—almost like a vacuum—was around me instantly. But then I could hear the gurgling of the river as it pushed its silt-laden waters ever seaward. Some ravens made their presence known, and there were some other birds which I didn't recognize. The cool breeze that drifted down from the glacier filled my nostrils and lungs with the clean smell of snow and ice on this beautiful August morning. I knew then that all the dreams I'd ever had about flying in the North had been fulfilled with this one simple act of acquiring my own airplane. The cost suddenly became irrelevant! "Now, if I could just learn to fly the darn thing," I thought as I climbed in to head back to Kent's so he wouldn't worry.

Flying lessons come in all shapes and sizes and can come at any time. I got one right then because the engine refused to start. Soon, I was outside turning the propeller by hand because the battery was the first thing to give up. "Probably not enough flying time with all this starting and stopping," I thought. When gas started dripping out of the carburetor, I knew this was not going to be easy but at least it was getting fuel, my Dad's mechanical lessons coming to the rescue once again. But now I had to be extremely careful as fully-primed aircraft engines have a way of running away from their starters, which was me in this case, and I was standing on a gravel bar in the middle of nowhere. I hated to think of how many times I would have to wade (or swim) the many branches of the Knik to make my way back to the Butte to say nothing of the grief I'd cause Kent and his family since I had told no one where I was going. A lot of lessons about flying and airplanes were being crammed into my head all at once it seemed.

I was doubting that my aching cranking arm could take much more when it coughed. Aaa! Almost. And it fired off the next try. When I was airborne again, I could hardly believe an hour and a half had slipped away.

Kent was nervous all right, but figured I had gone up on the river. He had enough savvy to understand about delays but warned me about leaving flight plans. I got the message.

Caribou Creek was about ninety miles up the Glenn Highway and back into the hills. They showed me on the Anchorage chart where we would be going—a gold mine that several partners and Kent would be working the following summer which had a strip on it. Some of the machinery and equipment had already been hauled to the site.

Since Kent and I got started before the others, we had a chance to look around the area some before going to the mine. Being that close to mountains was a new experience for me in an airplane. I'd been through quite a few with a helicopter, but this Cub didn't land vertically and I wondered how I was going to manage the gorge landing by the mine as we flew past. I missed seeing the wolf that Kent tried to point out to me as it sped into the trees, but the bear's glistening brown coat could not be overlooked as we climbed up out of the valley to the open hillsides above the claims. Grizzly bears always sent a prickling sensation through my bones, and when I saw the big Dall ram another thousand feet or so above him, I knew we were in real wilderness.

Again, the satisfaction of just being there and being a part of all this was somehow enough. They say nothing comes to you until you are ready for it. Well, I was, and so was every fiber in my being if the tingling I felt was any sign.

Of course, it may have been the coming landing that had me on edge. At least, it should have. The strip was right down on the river where the canyon narrows to run through a deep gorge some distance below the claims. It was wide enough to get down and take a look before making a commitment, and I was glad because this was a one-way strip. You land upstream around the dog-leg and take off down — right towards the cliffs and disregard the wind unless it got your attention. The elevation was twenty-five hundred feet and I knew it would take extra power, but didn't realize just how much until we almost clipped the trees going upstream on our first pass.

Kent was silent in the back. On the next try, I dragged it in and set it down. My fingers and armpits were wet with perspiration. I wondered how many flying lessons a body could absorb like this and was glad there would be some others there soon who could show me the whys and hows of getting out of there. From the ground, the cliffs looked ominous but the view was spectacular. I was in the Alaska I'd waited for all my life.

Does everybody's neck hair stand up when they find their first flake of gold? Another new dimension was added to an already tingling body that was taking on too much too fast, I feared.

When Stan, Dan, and Randy arrived, bringing the others, there was hardly room to park all the airplanes. I realized then that the advice I'd been given so many years before about learning to fly and figuring out a way to own my own airplane couldn't have been more right on. I was almost reluctant to head down the road to Wisconsin. Of course, I hadn't gotten out of Caribou Creek yet.

The one thing that I was beginning to understand about flying in the bush was that you had to be gutsy. That is totally different from being foolhardy. Maybe gutsy is not the correct term. What seems to happen, though, is that your confidence builds as you experience

more and more. Each time you stretch your limits adds
to that confidence. Hopefully one doesn't stretch so far
he breaks something in the process...like his head, or in
this instance...my head.

When I started down the Alaskan Highway toward
Wisconsin, it was not that I was completely inexperienced
about the whole thing. I'd done it twice before but in
reverse order and from slightly different starting points.
But now I was on my own entirely and I knew enough to
be cautious. Before leaving Anchorage, James Clyde,
who had also quit the helicopter business by this time,
sat me down and talked me through every conceivable
radio transmission I'd encounter from Merrill Field to
the farm in Wisconsin. Jim was now an FAA flight
controller at Elmendorf AFB.

"Listen," he said, "don't let anyone intimidate you
along the way. You are the captain. You tell them your
intentions. You don't have to ask their permission for
anything." It was nice to talk with someone who had
worked both sides of this flying business. Jim was a pilot
first and a controller second and eventually got out of
the tower and back into a cockpit where he knew he
belonged all along.

So I was not entirely unprepared to tackle the highway
alone. I did want to keep the airplane a surprise to everyone
in Wisconsin, so I filed all my flight plans with Palmer as my
home base, having given Kent all the pertinent Wisconsin
telephone numbers and other information he would need in
case something did happen.

A Super Cub has about 350 miles of range and
usually you are pretty glad to get out and stretch and
head for the john by then anyway. Flying at 100 mph,
plus or minus any wind, translates into a lot of time on

your butt no matter how you look at it or how beautiful the scenery is that is slipping past. To make the 3500 to 4000 miles in three or four days, if you have good weather to start, requires being airborne before the sun and stopping to refuel at least three times during the day—maybe more. No matter, after two days of that kind of schedule, your hind-end is beginning to think your head must be disconnected because it's a long, confining ride.

After a few trips, (I'm now on my eighth) the scenery and the gas stops become almost routine. Whitehorse, Yukon, is a real place now and not something from Robert Service's poems. I noticed on the chart once that Lake Laberge wasn't that far out of the way and it, too, became fixed in my memory. There have been side trips into the Northwest Territories from Watson Lake. The South Nahanni River and Virginia Falls are real places, too. Once I took the gorge route and ended up in Spokane but stopped at Hudson's Hope, B.C. to soak up some of the atmosphere that Bradford Angier had written so much about.

Crossing the Rockies was always a challenge. The locals call it "flying the rock" and more than once I've had to s-t-r-e-t-c-h my experience—once by flying at night for a couple of hours. This is taboo in Canada without an instrument rating, by the way, but it got me out front of a fog bank that was moving into the area and possibly would have grounded me for days.

My experience continued to grow. When the right magneto acted up in Grande Prairie on that first solo trip, I was glad I'd spent the time with James Clyde. "You'll have to go into Edmonton International to get it repaired," the mechanic said. I'd avoided the larger airports wherever possible, but now I was being forced

Diane
Hill

to expand my experience level once more. Approach Control Radar vectored me to a straight-in heading on their active runway after giving me a couple of 90 degree turns so they could positively identify me.

"Negative on the transponder," I had said, trying to put some of James Clyde's authority into it with my initial transmission. It worked. They politely guided me around the jet traffic and eventually I was safely turning off the active and onto the taxi way, where they directed me to switch to ground control, who led me to the nearest FBO.

When I finally reached Wisconsin, it was close to supper time so I buzzed past our kitchen window before landing in our field. I later learned that my daughter had excitedly jumped up from the table saying, "That has to be my daddy. No one else would do that."

It was a much wiser pilot who stiffly crawled out amidst all the clamor of a daughter still jumping up and down, a wife shaking her head in disbelief and neighbors pouring down the lane to our house. Airplanes were much more of a novelty in Wisconsin than from where I had just come. I had surprised everyone, including myself, but I was truly grateful at the same time.

All the relatives and all the neighbors were extended the same invitation. I'd be glad to take anyone for a ride who wanted to go. The first one was on me. The second one would be highly negotiable. Before winter's snow covered the ground, I had given over 150 rides in the back seat of that little plane from our own bush field. Some folks in their seventies went into the air for the first time. It was a gratifying experience that has lasted throughout the years.

Heading to "work" the following spring took on a new meaning since I was now "driving" myself. I took along one of my wife's cousins for company, just to show him the sights. We had a great time, especially through Lake Clark Pass. The needle peaks and the ice blue skies with the turquoise water below, will be long remembered.

Since this was to be my first year to try fishing for herring, we had departed the Midwest in April and had arrived in Bristol Bay to see all the fish processors off shore waiting for the ice to go out. On the radio we overheard them talking back and forth to the aircraft that supported them.

"*Bering Bird*, this is the *Bering Star*. Over," someone was saying.

"Ted, isn't your boat called *Baldy*?" the cousin asked.

"Yes, why?"

"And now you have a "bird" to go with it," he answered. And so the name stuck. *Baldy Bird* it was and has remained, but there was still something unsettled.

After fishing season that year, a new diesel VW Rabbit found its way into my wife's garage and now *Baldy Bird* was truly the best single thing I'd ever done for myself.

But it is not always smooth along the roads we travel. A "mid-life crisis" would bring my marriage to its knees, and my life would change course once again.

chapter 8

It is dark on the tundra when I wake up. The wind gusts are no longer ripping at the tent fly but the rain continues—its gentle spattering a pleasant sound from inside the warmth of my sleeping bag. Whitney's breathing, deep and full, is from another world.

I'm wide awake but find I am too lazy to look for the flashlight so I can see my watch to know if I should go back to sleep or not. Civilization has a way of doing that. I smile to myself remembering that time in Canada when I woke in the middle of the night unable to go back to sleep because I didn't have a clock.

*   *   *   *   *

Before airplanes became a focus in my life, canoes were my true love. My early visions were always of the trapper or prospector or Indian family paddling deeper into the Canadian North to the land beyond the sky blue waters of the Quetico and on into the Arctic where the lakes and rivers teemed with fish and the waters were crystal to their bottoms. They would be living off the land as they went, sleeping under turned-over canoes as they camped at night. The canoes were always of birch bark or at least cedar and canvas, and the nights could have the Aurora Borealis showering down on them. Or rain, as it was on us right now. Waiting out a week of drenching weather under the canvas of a snug camp was not new to me. The sparks of evening fires brought a warmth that was probably more real in my mind than it was in fact.

I'd managed a few trips into this land I thought about so much over the years. I had the cedar strip, canvas-covered canoe and all the gear, and I was always looking for an excuse to go. Once I heard about a man and his wife up in Manitoba who lived so remote they only came out over the ice once every couple of years for supplies. I never found them, but it was a nice trip which I did alone. Another time, I visited Calvin Rutstrum, an outdoor writer of some fame, whom I had gotten to know. I took the train out of Sioux Lookout and had them let me off along a lonely stretch of tracks, canoe, packs and all. The silence that came down on me, as the last of the cars clicked their way around the bend and out of my sight, was awesome. I was totally alone and on my own but at peace with the world. I talked with myself about staying, but family obligations wouldn't let me. Rutstrum wasn't home when I got there, but it didn't matter. It was the trip that was important.

Always, I dreamed of someday paddling into a wilderness lake somewhere to a remote cabin and letting the lake freeze over behind me. When it melted in the spring, I would once again re-emerge into the world of man while paddling my trusty canoe back to civilization. It was a dream, I know, but it was always with me – even before Alaska seduced me to her bosom. A strange thing about dreams – if you hold them long enough and are willing to take that first step – they seem to come true. It's almost like magic. Unfortunately, they don't all come true the way you plan. I don't think anyone "plans" for a mid-life crisis.

The Davis' lived remote up on Lake Manitou out of Fort Francis. I had been there a couple of times in winter. The first time I drove my van over the ice road they maintained and used my canoe map to keep track of the many islands I passed until I got to their bay. The other time was the winter before when another friend and I had flown up in *Baldy Bird* to do some lake trout fishing through the ice at their place.

I knew Ted Davis had a trapper's cabin about four lakes to the east that was in bad need of repairs. He had told me that if I wanted to fix it up, I could use it any time. My ice-fishing friend and I visited it with the airplane while we were there. It certainly had possibilities! I got Ted on his radio telephone wondering if the offer was for real. "Sure!" he said. "Come on up!"

Three weeks later I crossed the border into Canada, my rather beat-up GMC camper loaded to overflowing. Two canoes, a small outboard with a side mounted bracket, gas, chain saw with a lumber maker attachment, a barrel stove, lanterns, cookware, my canoe tent, fishing gear and shot gun, and enough food and supplies to last for months, and of course – Big Red – my yellow labrador.

"He will be good company, Ted," my wife had said.

"Going up to do some hunting," I told the border guard who checked me into Canada as he patted Red on his head and scratched his ears. He never asked what was in the back.

I had made some deliberate decisions before setting out. For once in my life, I was going to let nature be the rule and the clock. When I was hungry, I would eat; when it got dark, I would sleep. Anyway, there would be no schedules to keep.

"You're not even taking a radio?" my high school chum who was now a doctor in San Francisco had asked when I told him about my adventure.

"No, because then I'd have to have a clock to know what time to listen to the 'bush messenger.' And besides, there would be batteries to worry about and the recharging, etc. etc.," I replied. "I intended to simplify my life. Besides, I packed all the classics that I've never gotten a chance to read. I won't be lacking in entertainment."

"Be careful, Ted. It would be tough sustaining a crush wound up there all alone."

"I will, Dave. Don't worry. At least I don't have my appendix to worry about," I added, trying to lighten up the conversation a bit. I didn't want to dwell on the what if's. I had enough other things to worry about already.

Vickers Lake was a winding sixty-mile drive east and north out from Fort Francis, Ontario, across the lower end of Rainy Lake and up the road towards Dryden. It was another quarter-mile hike through the spruce and yellowing aspens on a rather well-used portage trail to the water's edge. I arrived in early afternoon and decided to only pack the "junk" down to the water but sleep one more night in the truck. I would be leaving the pick-up at the landing when I got the cabin livable, but first, I wanted to re-check and make sure it hadn't disappeared or something. This was the first time I would be seeing the little cabin without snow, and I wanted to make a last minute list of what I'd need to repair the floor and the windows, which I knew needed some work, but I wasn't sure what else would need revamping. I'd even brought some jacks along to lift the logs on the front side of the cabin which I remembered had rotted and settled the cabin on a slight tilt.

The air was as crisp and clean-smelling as I had imagined all those years I'd read and dreamed of coming to this North Country. It took longer to get everything down the trail than I anticipated. Tomorrow, I would paddle into the wilderness to stay. Sleep did not come easy that first night with the butterflies in my stomach trying to get out for a look at the big October moon that had come up to welcome us to our new home. October! I squeezed my eyes closed even tighter. I needed some sleep.

Big Red had been in canoes since he was a pup when he replaced Buff, whom we lost to an infection some years before. He was the perfect movable weight to trim out the load so we rode evenly through the water. We took only the tent and camping gear on this first trip. The plan was to set up a camp and take stock of things and then return for the second canoe to haul the barrel stove and all of the tools I had managed to get across the border. I smiled when I remembered the guard petting Red who yawned and stretched as he awoke from his nap. Nothing seemed to excite Red. Not a care in the world. And he was no more excited now as he settled himself down near the bow. Red was content to stay where I told him and move when I asked. His only real desire was to be with me. He was the perfect companion.

The canoe glided effortlessly through these sky-blue waters. (Hamm's knew what they were talking about!) The shorelines were inverted in the mirror surface of the lake. A few ducks scampered back amongst the rocks on the near shore, reluctant to leave as we slid by. I smiled as Red eyed them only moderately. He never rushed into anything. Buff would have had us overturned in the water by now, but it was OK. Red was not to be outdone when it came to hunting.

The cabin was where the map said it was supposed to be, snuggled smoothly in amidst the spruce and aspens and the scattered birches. Its cedar logs were chinked with moss. Its back faced the north, which sloped up behind and into the trees. My bay was larger than I remembered, and the colors of the fall splendor surrounding it seemed strangely out of place. My only recollection was in winter, which would come soon enough, and there was lots to be done before then.

As soon as the tent was up and the camp was in order, I took a hard look at the cabin for the first time. The front bottom log had indeed crumbled, as I remembered, as had parts of the two side logs next to the ground. The 12 X 14 foot floor was a shambles and would need to be replaced completely. The screen door had fallen away from its broken hinges, and a window pane on one side was missing. Two others had holes in them and the roof needed some tar paper replaced, but it could have been worse. Certainly, I had my work cut out for me: My little lumber-making attachment for the chain saw would not be adequate for a project of this size. Oh, it might have been, but I was not here to make this a survival situation. I wanted to make the place as comfortable as I could before the snows finally came, and enjoy the experience at the same time. Still, it was obvious that I would have to head back to town and get some flooring.

But "town" now took on a new meaning. It meant paddling the seven miles back to the landing and securing the canoe upside down in the brush somewhere and then walking the quarter mile to where the truck was parked—hoping all the while that it started. There were still the sixty curvy miles through the once spruce-covered and now mostly logged-over countryside to drive through. Realistically, it was a three-hour trip just to get to town.

So....Red and I headed back into town the very first day we moved into the wilderness. The lumber yard was still open when we pulled in, and I said a silent prayer for that. The six sheets of 4 X 8 flooring fit well on the canoe rack and everything else went into the camper shell. As we started out of town, we stopped one last time at the Dairy Delight. No sense pushing this wilderness thing too far I figured. While I was finishing the last of my chocolate shake, Red was gulping the last of my hamburger—his pleading brown eyes having won out once again.

"Maybe we better swing back past the supermarket and get you another sack of food, huh, Red?" Eighty-three dollars later, not counting the flooring, we were again on our way into the wilderness.

It was nearly dark when we got back to the landing, so I decided to spend another night in the truck before heading to the camp on Vickers. Besides, I needed to start figuring out how to get everything that I had accumulated up the lake. For supper, I ate some chocolate chip cookies that I couldn't resist while in town, and washed them down with the last of the fresh whole milk I expected to taste all winter. Red ate his fill of the Purina dog chow we brought out to the landing with us. Sleep came a bit easier this second night with a great horned owl hoo, hoo, hooing to the moon. Tomorrow, we would move into the woods.

It took some ingenuity getting the 3/4 inch 4 X 8 sheets of compressed chipboard flooring to the water's edge by myself, but I made it. I rigged the two canoes catamaran-style, having cut the cross poles from the nearby spruce and attached the motor to the aluminum Grumman I'd borrowed for the winter. It made quite a stable platform for hauling the big load that was now stacked on shore.

With Red's nearly eighty pounds and my own one hundred and ninety, half the flooring and the barrel stove, plus some of the other junk which Mark Twain so aptly termed when he described civilization as *the limitless multiplication of unnecessary necessaries,* the load was barely manageable. The very stuff I wanted to experience life without had found its way to Vickers Lake. I was not quite as rugged as I thought, it seemed. But at least I'd be leaving behind electricity and clocks. It was a start. It took three more loads to get into the wilderness. But I was there at last.

Supper over an open fire, a cup of steaming tea and the walk down by the water to watch and listen as the evening settled in was prime time for me. Red, too, seemed to enjoy it. Normally, he wanted only to be lying against my knee and have his ears scratched, but now he sat intently nearby with his ears and eyes fixed on the mysterious sounds of the night. He was totally alert. Perhaps his wolf ancestors were out there somewhere in the night talking to him. It was for certain that he was tuned into something that was beyond me. I think Red had settled in, too, but on a different plane than my own. I was glad I had brought him along, and wondered if early man had felt the same way when he first made friends with the canine world.

Work on the cabin could only begin after I had completely dismantled and removed everything from inside. Once that was done, I set about tearing out the old floor and what was left of a kitchen pantry hidden under the floorboards. Restoring this "root cellar" of sorts made more and more sense as I dug through the rubble. Several relish bottles were still intact after nearly twenty winters, if the pencil marks on the cedar log walls meant anything. Regardless of how long the stuff had weathered the cold, I knew for a fact that no one had lived here since the stove had been stolen several years before, and certainly no one was here last winter when we came up ice-fishing and checked the place out for the first time. One winter was all I needed to preserve anything, but I wanted to fix it up as best I could for the Davis'. Yes, the root cellar/pantry would stay.

I had brought the railroad jacks along to raise the cabin so I could replace the bottom logs on the front but had second thoughts about that on closer examination. Had I been a carpenter, or had I possessed some experience along that line, I probably would have tackled it, but I had visions of the whole cabin crumbling down in a pile of sticks if I started moving things around.

The non-carpenter approach was to simply install the new floor on a level plane and disregard the sloping side wall logs. This involved considerable digging near the rear of the cabin before I could lower into place that first cross log I planned to use as a floor joist. It took some fudging here and there, but finally I got the five joists installed and ready to accept the particle board flooring. But before I could start nailing that down, there was another project I had to do.

I'd heard about bringing outside air directly to the wood stove in log cabins rather than having it sucking what it needed in through the chinking between the logs or wherever else it could to keep the fire burning. When you supplied the cold outside air directly to the stove, the warmed air inside the cabin would now be of a higher pressure and would push out through those same cracks that otherwise would have cold air streaming in to feed the stove. Thus you ended up with a cozy, draft-free living area. Sorry, Mr. Twain. Another unnecessary necessity, I know, but among the things I'd lugged into the wilderness was the piece of tubing along with the elbows and fittings to do the job. It would go under the floor and directly up to the stove.

After I dug out the tiny root cellar, I cut enough dry cedar poles to split and form into walls, with enough shelves to store all my simple needs next to the earth from which it all came in the first place. I was really beginning to get into "returning to my roots" by the time the floor was in place and the stove installed. There is nothing to compare with the pleasure of moving into a warm and snug cabin—even without the bunks—until you have slept for a month on the ground in a tent. And, although the tent had served me quite well, the dampness was coming through as the days continued to get colder. November had brought the first skiffs of snow and the days were decidedly shorter.

When my new spring pole bunk was finished, and the kitchen cabinets had been re-installed, something happened that made me realize that civilization was not going to leave me easily. I started waking up at night. Maybe it was the warmth of the stove, or maybe I was more relaxed somehow. The longer nights may have been part of it, too. But, after I ate supper and cleaned up the dishes, I'd write in my journal, or read by lantern light until my eyelids sagged. Sleep, when it came, was sudden and deep. When I awoke, I was as wide awake as I'd been tired the night before. But it would still be pitch black outside. Was it near morning and time to get started on a new day? Or was it only midnight, or had I been sleeping even less time than that? I wasn't enough of a woodsman to tell from the stars or the moon, and it wouldn't have helped much anyway with the clouds the way they were. Without a watch, I was lost and would lie there in the dark and wonder. Another of civilization's scars had been uncovered. On the morning of the fourth sleepless night, I broke through the thin ice sheets that now extended out from shore and paddled the *Old Town* once again to the road. Then I drove the sixty miles back to town and bought a battery-powered watch and slept like a hibernating bear from then on.

I had gone to the wilderness to experience many things. Living without electricity, running water, and indoor plumbing were the most obvious, but also I wanted to see what it was like being alone — really alone. I found out something very interesting. We are never alone.

There seemed always to be a voice within me, and I wondered if it was "the still small voice" that Eileen

Caddy had talked about in *The Magic of Findhorn*. She claimed that it was God talking to her, and I wondered if the Indian spirits were doing the same with me. I had known for some time in my life that I was more spiritually in tune with "The Great Manitou" than with my Protestant up-bringing, but I doubted that I had a direct line as Caddy had. Still, I was aware of things, subtle things, that never had occurred to me before I came to the woods. Smells from the slightest shift in the wind now got my attention. Or, paddling to a distant bay and finding nothing of particular interest, I might find upon my return that a moose had strolled past the cabin door. Perhaps these things were nothing, but I suspected these subtle urges were the vestiges of the same ancestral ties that bind all humankind into one brotherhood, the brotherhood Chief Seattle spoke of in his famous speech to our president when we took away the land that his people had known since time began. His message still rings with the tone of a higher being.

Red started acting differently as well. In the morning, when I'd open the cabin door to let him out, instead of bolting through the door, practically tearing off the plastic-covered screen as he would have at home, he stopped in mid-stride half-way out and looked around in all directions. Another cautious step, then another. He was intent on something I didn't sense, but I understood his reactions because of what was going on within myself much of the time. Finally, he would let his guard down and tear about in his normal exuberance. Had wolves been nearby during the night? I never found their tracks if they had been: Or was he tuned to the same spirits he saw at sunset when we sat down by the point at the end of each day?

Being alone had never bothered me, or so I thought. But when I became conscious of trying to be alone and not having any interactions with other humans, I was amazed at how many interruptions I actually had this far out in the bush. Moose hunters would paddle out of their way to say hello or ask directions if they saw me in a nearby bay gathering up dry cedar stumps for kindling. An occasional fisherman would do the same. Outward Bound, I have been told, deliberately schedules a three day solo into their program. They say it usually takes that long before an individual gets to really know anything about himself.

It seemed the Canadians were no different. At Vickers, I thought I would have ample opportunity to experience aloneness, but it took some effort. If it wasn't a passing hunter, a motorist would see me at the landing where my truck was parked if I happened to be down that way checking on it. "What time you got, Bud?" they would yell from their rolled-down window. I would have to smile, wondering if the "moccasin telegraph" had spread the news about my new watch. Keeping time in the bush was obviously more widespread than I had imagined.

"Five past ten," I'd holler back and they would drive on. Darn—only three words. Nothing else. But in my mind, another three-day cycle would begin. I feared I would have to become a hermit on my own lake if I wanted to be alone.

When Bob, the Indian trapper who worked for the Davis', showed up late one afternoon, ice had begun to close up most of the smaller bays on the lake. I'd met Bob both times I'd visited the Davis'. He was a loner. In town, alcohol had cost him his family and his teeth, but in the woods, he was Indian.

"Must be about three," he said looking to the west.

"Closer to four," I answered looking at my new watch which suddenly seemed old.

"Couldn't get back across North Bay with the ice that formed last night. Mind if I camp here awhile?"

"Not at all. Come on and bring your stuff into the cabin."

Bob had left one boat at Lake Manitou several days before and then hiked a portage trail to where he had a canoe cached on Beverly Lake. From there he had paddled and portaged over to Vickers, where he had the boat and motor he was using now to check on martin and beaver sign. He never mentioned where he had spent the last couple of below freezing nights.

And so I had a boarder to add to my solitude. There would be time to be alone later. I didn't mind this visitor, for I was grateful to get the chance to learn something from a "real" Indian. I didn't have long to wait. There was one question that had been bothering me since I had arrived at Vickers. It seemed that everyone who stopped to chat with me had a different answer, but Bob was the only one who could know for sure because he had once lived here.

"How much wood did it take you and your brother to heat this place the winter you stayed here?" I had read their pencil marks with great interest many times: Nov. 29th, -30, 6 beaver. Dec. 12th, 27 below, 1 wolf, 3 martin. etc. etc. The other guesses had ranged from ten to forty cords depending on whom I had talked with.

"I don't know," he answered, slowly pondering as if the question didn't make any sense to him.

"What do you mean, you don't know? Those are your writings on the wall, aren't they, when you stayed here the winter of '68 and '69?"

"I think it was about then," he answered.

"Well, how much wood did you burn?"

"I don't know," he said once more, but then added, "We just went out and got what we needed every day."

First lesson: Only the white man plans for tomorrow. The Indian lives today. I had a hard time after that making myself stack up firewood, when previously it seemed to consume much of my day. Since I had to rely on green wood mostly anyway, it suddenly made no sense to stockpile it. I'd just cut a tree down whenever I needed to. Oh, I did go around and drag in some dry stuff that was down on the ground before the snows came in ernest, but if it was hanging up off the ground, I let it be. I figured I had enough for a week if I somehow hurt myself. Probably a typical white-man syndrome of some sort.

Bob let me tag along to the beaver lodges he trapped. Fresh "black ice" had formed on the most protected waters now as winter's hand slowly settled over the area.

"Ever fall through?" I asked, looking down at the rocks and old stumps perhaps twelve feet below us as we crossed the east end of the bay in front of the cabin.

"No. When ice start to go down, I back up," he answered.

I noticed he poked the ice repeatedly with the stout pole he carried as we moved along. The cracking sounds were eerie — actually scary. Even Red was shaking after we coaxed him out on the thin ice. When it cracked, he tried to get as close to me as possible which was between my legs, and now we were even more scared because our combined weight on this precarious perch creaked with every step.

When we got to the marshy ground between lakes, Bob really probed the grass and brush under foot with his pole. "No warning in swamp. Just go through." He seemed to have reverted completely to his Indian English, and I wondered about that because he seemed too well-educated.

By the beaver lodge, however, his "real education" saved me from taking a dunking. He was showing me how to set snag hooks in a passageway near the beaver's winter feed bed. I started to walk around him to get a better angle for a photo and he grabbed my arm, stopping me short. "Don't walk there. Ice thin. Beaver swim there lots." He reached over with his pole and tapped the ice where I was about to step. Black, murky water spilled up from the tiny hole he had made and into the thin skiff of snow that had accumulated next to the lodge. When he measured to the bottom, I realized that I would have been three miles from the cabin and soaked to my belt had I gone in. The sun was out, but the thermometer hovered in the teens. At best, it would have been a miserable trip home.

The lessons were endless. On one portage, Bob waited for me. He was standing by a scarred cedar tree which bordered the trail. It had taken so much abuse over the years it was amazing that it still lived.

"Many moose pass this way."

Bob could say more in fewer words than anyone I knew. What he was referring to was, of course, only bull moose, whose horns happened to have clipped the cedar as they went from one lake to another. This was not a rub where they scratch the velvet off their horns each fall on some sapling prior to the rut. This was a fully mature, gnarled old cedar that had somehow withstood the parade of moose passing that way for who knows how long. All the cows and calves and immature bulls were apparently not included in Bob's few words. If you've ever witnessed a large bull crashing through the brush to get away from you and then try to follow him, you know they don't leave as much sign as you would expect. For this tree to be marked the way it was obviously impressed even the Indian.

Another time, going down Vickers Lake early one morning to check on my truck, we were scooting along with his boat and motor at five times what I could do in my canoe. Sitting in the bow, I was mesmerized by the stillness and the upside-down shoreline when suddenly the motor stopped. It took me a second to realize I was hearing a shell being clicked into a chamber.

"What's wrong?" I asked, as I turned to look at my Indian friend.

"Something swimming." His eyes were scanning the distant shore, but his finger was pointing out in front of the boat to a series of ripples so slight I had not noticed them distorting the upside-down trees I'd been so engrossed in watching. The rifle cracked in my ears, and I saw the thrashing splash and the otters at the same time. One started swimming away, but when it turned to look back, the rifle went off again. I saw the bullet strike the water, and if it didn't go between the otter's ears, it was darn close. He was down and gone instantly, having escaped by the thread on which all life seems to hang in the wild. When we retrieved the first otter, the .222 had cleanly punctured an eye. From a moving boat—I was more than just a little impressed.

At night, there was always something that needed attention besides cooking supper—an animal to skin and stretch, a packbasket strap to repair or traps to look after, and knives to sharpen. This gave us ample opportunity to sit by the stove and chat. It was during this time I would try to get Bob to tell me stories about his grandfather or something about his upbringing or anything, but he never understood what it was I wanted to hear. Unless I asked him a specific question, he was at a loss to express himself. I tried not to show my disappointment. I did learn that he had guided sport fishermen every summer since he was fifteen. He was frying up the northern pike we had caught on our way home that afternoon. "Ate fried fish every lunch every day all summer" since he could remember and never once got tired of it. "Mostly walleyes though," he added, referring to the status most Canadians placed on northerns. Jackfish were not the finest eating, but when Bob placed those first golden chunks on my plate, I knew why he never tired of fish.

As we traipsed through the brush each day, following the tracks we had made to the various traps he had set, I always wondered why he never chopped off the troublesome limbs or branches that we invariably had to crawl under or around. He had the axe in his hand, but I was beginning to learn something about Indians (or at least this Indian) — they never do anything they don't have to do. Walking through the woods was as natural to him as walking down a path was to me. I was the only one there who was out of place.

Another thing I noticed, Bob never once looked back to see where I was or if I was coming along. Not that it bothered me. I could handle myself OK, but still I wondered. He always carried the bulk of the trapping gear while I usually brought the lunch and camera and whatever else we might need. Red was along on these jaunts, too, and if we were coming to an area where Red could bumble into a trap, Bob would let me know long before we got there. I'd get a leash on Red until we were out of danger again. Other than that, Bob was always out in front, always had the biggest load, and always I could just barely keep up with him.

When a week had passed with the temperatures near zero every night, Bob announced he would go home the next day. First there were the hook sets we had to pull out of the beaver pond and some sort of a toboggan to make so he could drag his heavy pack along behind him across the new ice he knew he would encounter on the way over to Manitou. "Too much weight in one place if I carry everything on my back," he said. I was beginning to see how he managed to stay dry all these years. A true woodsman had everything worked out beforehand, which saved him considerable grief later on. There was no room for hot-dogging here, as this simple man had demonstrated time and again while he methodically went about his daily work. To make the sled, we scrounged around for some of the old floorboards I'd salvaged and stored along with some tin from the roof. This we nailed to the boards, after fastening cross-pieces in place for stability, thus forming a crude up-turned toboggan. Everything would now slide over the three inches of snow that had covered what ice had formed. The main part of the lake was still open, and Bob figured it would remain that way for another month.

The first snows had come rather quietly while Bob was there. We both had smelled it when we woke one morning. The weather had warmed up slightly, but it was black outside when Bob asked from somewhere deep within his sleeping bag: "What time is it?"

I smiled once again as I rummaged around for the flashlight. "Nearly five."

"Smell the snow?"

"I thought that's what it might be." I could feel the calm deep inside myself. Here I was snug in a cabin in the Canadian Northwoods, with winter finally catching up with me. I hadn't experienced being alone yet but figured that would come soon enough. Certainly, I had learned much about myself already.

Bob and I would use his boat and motor to haul his gear up the lake as far as we could get. Big Bay would probably be ice-covered by now, but not safe enough to walk over. Our plan was to get as far as we could in the boat, walk overland to skirt the most dangerous ice, and then hopefully pull the toboggan the rest of the way to the portage leading into Beverly, where he had stashed the canoe. From there, he would go on alone, pulling the canoe over the ice or paddling it, whichever worked out. Beverly Lake froze late as did Manitou. I would bring the boat and motor back to the cabin and store it under the eaves for the winter.

The new snow was brilliant and the sun beat down in vengeance as we started walking over to pull the last of the beaver sets. Bob had hooked two more beaver which made three in all from that pond.

"That's enough from here anyway. Need some seed for next year," he said as we started back to the cabin.

By the time we got the beavers skinned, I figured we were pushing our luck on daylight.

"I'll make it OK once I get to Manitou. I can find my way in the dark easily after that," Bob assured me. His civilized English had returned for the moment.

We got to Big Bay only to find that it was frozen out further than Bob had figured. The only place where

we could beach the skiff was on a rocky arm that protruded into the lake where the wave action had kept the water open. It was tough going at first, until we got past all the rocks and into the timber, but now I knew for sure what I'd been suspecting all along. Bob was carrying the heavy pack on his back plus the axe in one hand and his ice-probing pole in the other. I was toting the empty toboggan and my camera — practically nothing weight-wise — and yet I could barely keep up with the Indian. True to form, he never once looked back, but he *was* pacing me! He knew every minute where I was and how I was coming along. His lifetime of guiding had taught him how to cope with the green-horns he was continually around. Had he always been up ahead waiting on me, I'm quite sure my self-confidence would have been shattered long before. I had learned many things from this man, but the one that was foremost was: Don't underestimate anyone on his home turf!

We got to Beverly Lake and dragged the canoe Bob had cached there the week before onto the shore ice and loaded all his things aboard. He fashioned a towing bridle to leave his hands free and started tapping his way out to where the open water started. I sat down on a nearby rock and watched. We bid our farewells as he moved along, always thumping the pole into the ice ahead of him. Finally he stopped and backed up rather quickly. Now he was pushing the canoe. And then he was sitting down on the floor inside and humping it along with his body motion and pushing with a paddle until he slid down into the water. As he was about to round a bend and out of my sight, he turned and waved. I was alone in the Canadian wilderness at long last.

Darkness had overtaken us by the time Red and I hit the beach in front of the cabin. I wondered how Bob was getting along, but knew I didn't need to worry.

Now that stockpiling firewood seemed senseless, I filled my days with projects. I built shelves wherever they would fit: kitchen shelves, storage shelves, and book-shelves. I even built a chair using split poles. The engineering in such a project for a non-carpenter about overwhelmed me at first, but after several tries and considerable overkill, I had a very comfortable, very large, lean-back-on-the-rear-legs-as-much-as-I-please chair that gave me hours and hours of pleasure, both in the building and in the sitting. With my oil lamp hanging down from one of the ceiling purlins, I could read to my heart's content. Unfortunately, after a long day in the cold, my eyelids were more content to rest than I liked.

I had tucked a harmonica and an instruction booklet into my gear, thinking it would give me hours of pleasure when those long winter nights finally came. A musician I am not, and there is no one who knows it better than Red. As soon as I would get it out and wet my lips, Red would be up from his bed by the stove and sitting at my feet, his head cocked to one side waiting for the first notes to sound. Whether he was trying to accompany me or to drown me out with his mournful crying, I never was quite sure.

Red had learned to pull a small sled by now, thanks to Bob showing me how to get him started, and it was fun when the two of us went up through the lakes with Red pulling the sled with my pack instead of me having to tote it all the way. I still carried it over the portage trails though, because the going was a lot tougher there than out on the lakes. I learned to depend on Red to drag our fresh supplies in from the highway when we did go to town, and he seemed to enjoy having a job to do. Once though, on a particularly cold day, the GMC refused to start, and there was nothing to do but ski the seven miles back to the cabin empty-handed. Red even pulled me along as well the last few miles, because he knew there was some cooked beaver waiting for him when we got home. We both enjoyed the fruits of Bob's trapping, as did the Canada jays, who stayed around more and more now that they had a meat supply to pilfer. Red took to protecting his beaver carcass cache that we had hung outside on the cabin walls, and would sometimes lie outside the cabin door on sunny days and dare those pesky birds to come close. Red wanted to be part of everything I did, and if I didn't get him hooked back up to the sled fast enough after coming off a portage trail and out on the lake, he was there nudging my hand with his muzzle to remind me. Red also taught me much that winter. If we humans knew half as much about unconditional love as dogs do, it is awesome to think of the possibilities for the world.

Since I had no set schedule to follow nor anyone around to influence any of my daily activities, I'd sometimes declare a holiday and spend the entire day engrossed in a book or writing in my journal. And although my winter days were filled, it was a lonely existence, too. When it got close to Christmas, I knew I had to leave the woods. Ted Davis and Bob had flown in to check on me about a week before. I had the cabin decked out with a bright red ribbon on a balsam wreath on the door and candles in all the windows, but I knew it was time to say goodby to this place. They were all going to town to be with family and friends and agreed to stop by with their snow machines and drag my loaded canoes to the road when they did. I had managed to be alone only twelve consecutive days in the nearly three months since I had come to live in the wilderness. Not long by most standards, but it was enough for me. Christmas was the time to be with family and friends.

chapter 9

The tundra conjures up many impressions among all who experience it in any of its moods, but the one thing that remains constant is the endless horizon — it is always there — just out of reach. Like being out on an ocean, the horizon is all you see until you look closer. Lost, no one is likely to find you in either place. And the sunsets can be so beautiful that you can be lulled into thinking there is no danger, but both of these beautiful places can kill.

Whitney has camped throughout the world but always had a degree of control over where he was or what he brought along to smooth the way: The gear, the food and certainly the place. But here he took what was offered and had to make do. We both did. There were no cooking utensils save the one tin pail and two cups and two spoons I had along in the survival gear. It certainly made for simple dishwashing and would have made even Thoreau and Mark Twain happy.

A new meaning came to the term "charbroiled" as we laid the first of the Arctic graylings directly on the burning embers of the willow fire. Later, we peeled away the blackened skin and grabbed at the hot white flesh with our fingers and then ate the skin as well.

No fish ever tasted better, except perhaps Chu's charbroiled tuna bellies, which I had once on board the *Pacific Princess* somewhere off the coast of New Guinea. I was there, on a lark, once again, to fly a helicopter out in the middle of the Pacific where the only place to land was on a tiny platform that moved with the whims of the sea. I was chasing tuna in the winter then as a diversion from the salmon fishing that had occupied my summers for so many years. What I was really looking for was to get a good suntan for once in my life.

* * * * *

"Ted, you don't do a darn thing in the winter. Why don't you go and fly the helicopter off one of those tuna boats down in the harbor?"

It was Gene Golles giving me another razzing from his San Diego living room. I'd stopped in to say hello near the end of a winter of traveling throughout the southwestern U.S. Gene was one of my oldest fishing friends from Alaska's Bristol Bay. We dated all the way back to the skiffing days and had both come a long way over the years. He now had his wife up there with him, so I'd known them both a long time and felt comfortable staying with them a few days when they insisted. I was about to head back to Alaska when he told me about the helicopters and the tuna boats.

On my way out of town, I stopped along the waterfront in downtown San Diego, and there they were: Probably the most beautiful and certainly the longest seiners I'd ever imagined. Years before, I fell in love with the sleek 42 foot Kodiak Deltas that fished the herring runs in Togiak. But these were 220 footers. Eleven hundred ton capacity super seiners. Sleek giants of the sea. True ocean-going vessels that would stay out in any kind of weather until their fifteen enormous fish holds were stuffed with the frozen tuna that helped to feed a large portion of the world. Beautiful ships in every respect. But high overhead on the upper-most part of the flying bridge, nearly three stories above me, was the most beautiful ship of all — the helicopter.

I'd been in love with choppers longer than boats, except, of course, for my *Old Town* canoe. Helicopters did the impossible — ten thousand moving parts, all trying to come apart at the same time, and yet it flew. But more than that — it hovered. My T-shirt said it all: "To fly may be heavenly but to 'hover' was divine." I hadn't been around helicopters much since I started commercial fishing, but the desire was always there.

Just the thought of going on a South Pacific fishing cruise had my heart pounding. But to have a helicopter under my command at the same time had to be the adventure of a lifetime.

I could feel my senses shifting into the search and secure mode. I'd learned years before that what you know is not nearly as important as who you know, and I set about right then getting to know someone who knew something about helicopters and tuna boats. Fortunately, I've never had any trouble talking to people and soon found my way onboard the *Conquistador* chatting with anyone who would talk. The fact that I was a helicopter jockey and an Alaskan fisherman certainly made it easier. Soon I was being shown around the engine room and the galley and even the captain's quarters. When we climbed to the top most deck to check out the bird, I was hooked.

But I was also on my way back to Alaska. All I could really do was to jot down a few names of possible contacts and do whatever I could once I got North. By the following Christmas, I knew I was not going to get on a tuna boat from Alaska. The resume I sent out and the countless phone calls were not producing. I would have to go back down to San Diego in person and try again.

Before leaving Alaska, I stopped in at Wilbur's flight school on Merrill Field and bought a couple of hours of instruction in their old Bell 47 just to get the feel of being in a chopper again. It proved to be the best move I could have made since starting all this tuna stuff.

The Golles' were gracious enough once again to let me use their place as a base. I had given myself thirty days to get on a boat or give it up. I wasn't planning to sacrifice my own fishing business by getting myself stuck out at sea somewhere. When the salmon started their migration back to Alaska's shores in June, I planned to be there to intercept as many as I could.

It took three thousand miles of driving around California, and several hundred dollars in phone calls, but on my twenty-seventh day, I was on my way to the tiny island of Samoa in the South Pacific. I would be flying a helicopter off a tuna boat at last. Persistence does pay off sometimes. Perhaps that isn't the correct term. Luck has much to do with everything, and being a little gutsy doesn't hurt either.

Ultimately, I was standing in Bud Levitt's office for the umpteenth time when the telephone rang. Avey Gonzolves, the fish captain for the *Pacific Princess*, needed a pilot and needed one right now. Bud put his hand over the receiver and asked, "You got Bell 47 time?"

Had I not spent the past three weeks tracking down every lead, every phone number, and every hint of an opportunity of getting on a boat to always come up against the same question of how much time I had, I probably would have qualified my yes answer. My total flying time more than met tuna boat requirements, but my helicopter experience did not. Avey and I talked a few minutes to more or less get the feel of each other. I did not waste any time informing him that I'd done most of my 2500 hours of flying in Alaska but started spraying (crop dusting) with a Hiller 12-E in Oregon years before. I was forty-six and now had my own fishing business in Alaska but had never been on a tuna boat.

"How about Bell 47's? You flown them?"

"Sure, no problem," I said knowing I was stretching the most of the two hours I had at Wilbur's. Sometimes you can make yourself sound more confident than you are, but I hadn't lied. There was no problem or at least Wilbur's hadn't mentioned any.

We met for coffee the following morning. Avey showed up in his opened-necked shirt with his dark tan and gold chains and rings everywhere and driving his bright red, thirty grand Porsche. Fortunately, he was fifteen years my junior, so I grabbed at the opportunity to let him know I must have been flying since he was a little boy. He never did ask me straight out how much time I actually had in a Bell 47.

"We will be leaving in a few days. Probably Monday or Tuesday," Avey said when I quizzed him. I gave him Golles' number and got his. It was Friday.

"I'll be ready!" I said as we shook hands and went our separate ways. The instant he was out of sight, I headed for the telephone. Somewhere in my travels these past weeks, an ad for learning to fly a Bell 47 (D model) had caught my attention. "$800 for ten hours of instruction." Fortunately, I had jotted down the number.

It was in Riverside, California nearly two hundred miles away.

When the instructor answered the phone, I felt comfortable explaining the situation I was in. No matter what, I had to learn to fly that 47 this weekend.

"Come on up and we'll give her a go," he said.

I was there that evening and handed over the $800. We only had time to get some preliminaries out of the way and would start first thing in the morning. Two and a half hours into the instruction, he stopped me. "Look, Ted, to be honest with you, I can't teach you how to land on a tuna boat without one to practice on. You fly the helicopter fine so I'm going to give you the rest of your money back. Good luck."

As I was about to pack up and leave he added, "Oh yeah, let me know how it goes out there. I've always wanted to try that myself sometime."

It was a nice gesture on his part, giving me the money back like that, and it certainly helped my sagging confidence which had taken a downturn when the reality of what I'd gotten myself into actually took hold. Here I was about to go half way around the world and into the southern hemisphere where I'd never set foot, to be with people I knew nothing about, to fly a helicopter off a tiny, moving platform on which I had no experience.

Pago Pago (pronounced Pongo Pongo) is about as far from the Hawaiian Islands as they are from Los Angeles, in about the same general direction. A speck on the charts surrounded by blue in all directions. For the first time in my life, even though I'd studied navigation in two fields, I would be concerned with latitude and longitude for real. The Pacific Ocean, as I was soon to learn, was indeed one big hummer.

The *Pacific Princess* was even more beautiful in its tropical setting than were those first seiners I'd seen back in the States. However, the Bell 47 looked as though it had taken a direct hit in the Korean War, except for the fact that the G-2 models with the high individual gas tanks behind the bubble didn't exist then. It had sustained a tail boom strike while chained down to its perch on the last trip. They had encountered a tropical storm during the night and the main rotor tie downs had snapped, letting the blades begin to turn freely, picking up momentum as the winds increased. Evidently, with one of the crashing swells, the *Princess* had shuddered hard enough when it hit the wave to cause the main rotor blade to strike the tail boom — a nearly always fatal situation had it actually happened while being airborne.

Two mechanics had been flown in from New Zealand to put it back together. They were the first Kiwis I'd ever met and we got along marvelously well right off, and I was soon saying *G'day Mate* as well as they. Since some of the parts hadn't arrived as scheduled, there was time to get in some early morning swimming and to get acquainted somewhat with the activities that were going on in the harbor at what seemed a feverish pace.

At least ten seiners were there, but some were not fishing. Something about a cutback on the price of tuna and there not being the markets of a few years prior. It seemed everyone had a net-mending needle in his hand as the huge seines were being off-loaded or put aboard, depending on what status of repair they were in. When I inquired about their size, I began to realize that I had gotten myself involved in something that was hard to fathom. Nearly a mile long and hanging five hundred feet down into the water, the seines weighed nearly a hundred tons and were worth a million dollars. Add to the cost of the net a boat valued in the ten million dollar range and all of a sudden my little 32 foot operation in Alaska seemed insignificant. On the world scale, fishing was an unbelievably huge business. But it was the afternoon tropical showers and the evening breezes that I enjoyed most about being there.

Samoans, Peruvians, and Portuguese were involved in most of the activities, and I had heard that we would be competing with the Japanese and the Poles as well. Our navigator had even fished tuna off the coast of Africa, and on board, we had Chu, a master Chinese chef. I was truly at some kind of an international crossroads out here on this tiny island so far from anything I knew. The language mixtures and the catchy melodic music playing on all the open-windowed busses and the different races all had one thing in common — everything was measured in American dollars. It hadn't always been that way. Fine mats used to be the symbol of wealth here before this became an American Colony and big business pushed its way in. The tuna boats were here because Star Kist had built a cannery here in this beautiful natural harbor where the palm trees swayed and the beaches had the first signs of pollution with the litter that washed up each morning. They moved their San Diego operations to avoid the high American labor costs and were now no doubt taking advantage of a people who annually could live on three thousand dollars.

The repairs on the 47 progressed more rapidly than its initial condition indicated. I did what I could to help but spent much of my time talking with the other pilots about what I could expect once we put out to sea. Avey had said he would let me practice in the harbor before we sailed, but I had learned long before that to cover your own butt in all situations was smart business. I was glad I did.

Pilots are members of a fraternity of sorts — especially if you are not afraid to admit that you're scared. Everyone who flies has known fear at one time or another. How we all handle that fear is another matter. No pilot ever failed to open up to me in response to questions I had regarding something I was unsure about. Landing on a tuna boat at sea was an unknown to me. The pitching of the boat as it plowed its way along through the waves at the standard thirteen knots, sometimes moving up and down as much as ten feet or more while rolling from side to side was not to be underestimated in the least. "Be careful" was the common denominator in every conversation I had on that subject.

At 1:32 p.m. on February 3rd, the *Pacific Princess*, its side thrusters churning, eased away from the dock in Pago Pago and sailed past the other islands of Western Samoa. It then pointed its bow to the northwest and sailed on into the night. I had flown the helicopter to the perch on deck where it was now secuely chained the evening before, minutes after it came out of the repair shop, and so now had a single landing to my credit. The *Princess* unfortunately was still firmly fastened to the dock at the time. Avey had forgotten about the practice session he had promised in his rush to get underway. We sailed on into the night a second time.

Ships are much different than boats. I don't know for sure where the definition of one ends and the other begins, but I would suspect it is in the brain. Certainly, someone who sailed many years on this 250,000 ton monster and then came on board my 32 foot *Tin Can* would know he was on a boat. The same would be true, I'm sure, of an old navy captain who, after spending years aboard a destroyer then shipped out on the 220 foot *Pacific Princess.*

To me, I was on board one of the most beautiful ships in the world and taking the South Pacific cruise of a lifetime. The tropics. I had been to Hawaii once but this was as far south as I'd ever been. The Southern Cross had to be pointed out to me. The North Star which I'd looked up to my whole life, now guided the other half of the world. Here, below the equator, if water really did swirl down the drain the other direction, what would it do right on the line? If I got the chance, I would find out.

We had another imaginary line out in front of us somewhere as well. Off to the west was the International Date Line, where you could sail into tomorrow, today, and back again into yesterday if you wanted. There was going to be no shortage of things to learn here, provided, of course, I could learn to land the chopper back on its high perch while we continued to roll our way through these beautiful, blue, shark-infested waters where the horizon never changed. Always, it was there stretching on endlessly over the curve that sailors once knew to be the end of the earth.

We were now well clear of any landfall that could be reached with the chopper. Once off the deck, I would have one hour and forty-five minutes to figure how to get it safely back on board before getting into the fifteen minutes of reserve fuel that everyone had cautioned me to guard with my life. At most, I would have two hours before the engine quit.

"Warm it up, Ted." Avey's voice came over the ship intercom. He finally remembered our practice session the morning of our third day. The procedure was simple enough. First, the call would come over the speakers throughout the ship. I'd drop whatever I was doing and head to the top deck to be met by Filipo, the Samoan boy who would be responsible for hooking and un-hooking the tie-down chains whenever we arrived or departed. Together, we would do any last-minute items like untying the main blades and tail rotor. I'd check the oil and fuel once more and then climb aboard while getting into my May West and then buckle myself in. Filipo would then remove the doors and secure them safely below the deck before giving me the thumbs up sign that it was all clear to start the engine to warm it up. Avey would show up a few minutes later and buckle himself in but would never put on the May West.

"He was the captain and could do as he pleased," I thought. But if this bucket of bolts hit the water, even though we carried a life raft, flares, a special homing beeper, and other electronic gear if we were unconscious in the water, none of it would be worth a darn. At least, I wanted to be floating.

In Alaska, just going into the water meant almost certain death from exposure unless you got into your survival suit. Here, we flew in our shorts and sandals – the 85 degree water so inviting you almost wanted to be in it. This was different all right but surviving a ditching at sea in a aircraft was not something to be taken lightly. And even though the helicopter was equipped with pontoons, my experience landing on water with them was nil, but that of course was the lesser of my problems. To date, I had zero experience either flying off of, or landing on a boat while it was at sea. Period!

When the engine temperature hit the green and I'd checked the mags, I nodded to Filipo and he unfastened the back chain on my side and walked around in front of the bubble and did the same on Avey's side. We were half ready to go. The sweat streaming down my sides and soaking my flying gloves was not from the tropical heat. We still had two more chains to loosen.

Meanwhile, I checked in with Father John down in the wheelhouse via the radio. He was the master on board and carried all the legal papers to operate in international waters. He had thirty-five years at sea and a wife and seven kids at home, and would be our only link back to the boat once we left. As we made the radio checks he gave me the wind direction and its speed. He asked which way I wanted him to steer the ship to best take advantage of our own thirteen knots we were making as we plowed through the gentle swells on this tropical sun-filled morning. There was nothing on the horizon except the gentle curve of the earth.

The old Bell 47 had all it could do to develop enough horsepower with its reciprocating engine — even at red line to get off the deck if it was especially hot and muggy and there was no wind. And even though some turbulence was created as our own thirteen knot wind slammed into the ship's structure, it was safer to have this added breeze than not on most days.

So when the engine was warmed and the radio checks were completed, I shifted my gaze to the wind sock out on the bow and watched the oncoming swells. Father John watched the wind sock as well, and kept the bow of the *Princess* pointed accordingly. Usually, a couple of big ones would slam us and then it would smooth out a bit. I nodded to Filipo, who was squatting in front of the bubble plugging his ears with his fingers against the engine's noise. He quickly jumped up and removed the last chain from my side and from Avey's;

then he gave us the all-clear sign and left the deck. I visually checked to see that my side was clear of the chains by leaning out the door and looking and gave Avey the thumbs up. He then did the same for me. Leaving a chain attached when in a hurry to leave the deck was an invitation to die. There is a thing in helicopter circles known as a dynamic roll-over. It is technically difficult to explain and, once initiated, even more difficult to correct, with very few pilots being quick enough to react. Simply put, it meant auto-rotating back to the deck which you never left in the first place. As I said, it was complicated and was much easier to avoid in the first place by double-checking the chains.

When I got Avey's thumbs up signal, I pulled the collective and gently pushed forward on the cyclic. We rose off the deck and over the port side in one swooping motion. The old G-2 had done that many times over the years, and as we moved away on that invisible ocean of air and I looked back, the giant 220 foot, 1100 ton capacity super seiner that had appeared so massive at the dock was transformed into a boat and a tiny one at that.

Like it or not, my first lesson in landing on a moving platform at sea was underway. I had talked with everyone I could find who knew anything at all about what I could expect to happen once I left the ship, but nothing had come close to preparing me for this moment. I had put my life on the line once more and could feel its vibrance pulsing within me. Even my soul was totally committed.

Completing a wide circle out in front of the *Princess*, I could sense that every one of the remaining eighteen souls on board were glued to every porthole and rail on the starboard side to watch the newcomer from Alaska attempt his first landing.

Once more, the massive bulk of the ship was there as we eased up close, hovering just out of reach of its steel

Diane Hill

and aluminum sides. Here, it wasn't submissively tied to its berth at the dock. Free and at sea, it was a vibrant creature. Crashing through the swells, it sent spray and foam pulsing up from its gracefully curved bow as it plowed ever forward. From the vantage point of a helicopter hanging magically in thin air just inches from its grasp, the sight was menacing. By hovering level along its edge like that, it was easy to measure the height of the swells as the top deck rose above our pontoons only to pitch back down as the ship's hull plunged once more into the mile-deep blue water below us. And I could see the slight roll I'd been told about as Father John drove the *Princess* into the breeze that had come up from the south. The wind sock was holding true for a diagonal landing across the deck that was required to miss the twenty-six antennas that sprouted from all points aft. I knew how many there were because I had deliberately counted them during my worried long wait for this moment.

Tuna boats are all equipped with a high mast to handle the gear booms and the bird's nest, where two observers were stationed every daylight hour of every day. I knew they had the best seats in town for the show at hand, but as long as I could keep the chopper out in front of them and down on the deck, all would be OK. The problem was how to get over the edge of the pitching, rolling platform without catching a pontoon while hovering at the same speed as the *Princess*. The trick, I had been told, was to aim for and hit the small red-circled "T" that was painted on the platform. Everything else was supposed to fall into place after that.

Your entire concentration was supposed to be focused on that small "T"—almost. There was still the helicopter to fly: RPMs to monitor, manifold pressure to note, the turbulence of the air coming across the deck, and the edge of the deck itself that never once stopped coming up to grab a chunk of us as we hung there waiting and calculating for the right moment. A technique had been developed that helped overcome all this, but it took experience which I didn't have. Still, we all have to start from somewhere and I'd already been airborne for nearly fifteen minutes as the clock methodically ticked away at our precious fuel supply.

The technique, as it was explained to me, was to focus your eyes totally on the tiny red circle, making it your whole immediate world. Everything else you had to sense rather than actually see. By focusing on the circle, your brain automatically would transform it to an immovable landing zone much as a runway would be on land, where your eyes then are actually focused on the horizon. If you looked at the horizon here, the boat would drive out from under you, bringing along all its antennas, mast, and booms. It could more than ruin your day.

The time had come. I positioned the helicopter a few feet above the highest point that the deck was pushed skyward by the swells, and hovered diagonally along, keeping pace with the boat but now with my attention focused totally on the spot. When the *Princess* reached its apex on what I calculated to be one of the smaller swells, I headed for the little red "T" in the center of the circle and never once took my eyes away for a second, almost feeling my way there. The idea was to be solidly down on the deck before it started it's next upward thrust. Ideally, meeting it on the way down gave you the softest landing. If for some reason, you hurried this whole procedure, you would likely overshoot the spot. The rule then was to go around. It is one of the most prudent rules in aviation.

On my fifth go around, Avey says, "Want me to show you how I do it?"

Now, I knew that Avey did not have a license to fly, but dual controls were common in all the tuna choppers I'd seen. It is always nice to be able to give someone else the controls so you can take a break now and then.

"Yes. By all means." I was only too glad to be able to pry my fingers loose and let some warmth come back into them once again. My armpits may have been dripping but in my fingers was the cold reality of what was happening all around me.

Avey had tons of hours in the chopper from a string of pilots over the years who had been willing to give him lessons. He made it look deceptively easy. I had been hurrying over that terrifying edge much too quickly to be under control in time to hit the spot. "Av" gently set her down right on the "T".

"So that's how it's done," and off the deck we went once again. This time I swallowed hard and dragged us over the edge. The landing was a little rough, but I hit dead-center in the middle of the ocean on top of that tiny red circle with the "T" in the center. My first successful landing at sea was now history. But it never would get easy. Later, I would hear myself giving the same warnings that I had gotten when anyone approached me about flying for a tuna boat. "Be careful" was about all I could tell them.

Time, as we normally think about it, stops when you are at sea. The neverending routine turns days into fuzzy recollections. Soon only weeks are distinguishable and then only by some major event that has happened. And then you start to think in months. The latest *Playboy* calendar pin-up girl is the prime indicator of the date change as your thoughts concentrate more and more on the loved ones left behind. The picture frame in our minds is frozen on that last image, where it flickers constantly as we wait for the projectionist to unstick the film. Everyone was anxious, but finally the order was given and the *Princess* turned east. The trip was over — almost.

Two more weeks would pass with the big twelve cylinder locomotive engine pounding away all day and all night, as it had done every day and every night since our departure, its din and vibration now driven deeply into everyone's subconsciousness. I was the lucky one, though, because I had 350 hours of relief out on that still illusive horizon, but always, even there, there was engine noise banging into my ears. Yet I was grateful it was not otherwise.

There is far too much idle time on board for the pilot when flying is not required and so I had tried to help the crew sort fish whenever we made a big haul, but found I wasn't welcomed back there among the swirling net and flying chain as our fish holds slowly began to fill. Finally, the engineer took me aside and explained what was going on.

"Look, Ted, there are lots of workers on this boat but only one flyer. If you get slammed across the head with a chain, we'll have to take you back into a port somewhere and then find another pilot. That could easily add a month to an already long trip as it is — so stay out of their way."

When we turned east that final time, the crew was issued scrapers, wire brushes, and paint. The *Princess* would get a face lift before she sailed back inside the safe confines of Pago Pago once more. Rust and paint chips clung to sweaty muscular bodies as they clambered into every corner on deck and up every boom while the tropical sun burned down on us all. I thought to myself, "Well boys, if you refused my help once, you certainly don't need it now." And so I headed for the top deck with my beach towel and sun tan lotion. When the helicopter was spotless and shrouded for the last time, I spread out my towel, oiled my rounding body, and waited for my South Pacific cruise to come to an end. When we pulled up to the dock on the afternoon of May 6th, my skin was as dark as any Samoan's and unfortunately nearly as large. And although Chu's dinner of barbecued tuna belly was the finest meal I'd ever tasted, I was more than ready to have my feet on solid ground. In all, we had been at sea 3 months, 3 days, 1 hour, and 37 minutes.

chapter 10

I am sitting on the bluff overlooking the valley stretching out below our camp. It is misting again as evening closes in on this isolated place. We've been here always, it seems, but the crude log says we are still in our fifth day.

Whitney has hiked up the mountain behind camp where *Baldy Bird's* engine decided to quit on us. I know he wants to look over the gravel bar I didn't land on and perhaps quiz me why, but he is too polite to say so. Again, I am thankful to be here with such good company and grateful to have had all the opportunities in my life to be in so many remote and beautifully rugged settings as this one.

It is hard, though, to look at *Baldy Bird* and not wonder at how bad all of this could have been. The pact we had together has been fulfilled because I did walk away from it when the engine quit, and I have no regrets. I guess I've had my share of mishaps out flying in the bush, but they only seem significant to those who are looking in from the outside. I still get a bit annoyed at people, reporters in particular, and their comments about "crazy bush pilots."

* * * * *

After more than twenty-five years around airplanes, with much of it spent in Alaska's outback, if someone were to ask me today to define a "bush pilot," I would be hard pressed to give him an answer. I could tell him this about myself, however; "Sometimes, after being bounced around in turbulent wind gusts most of a day, trying to get a group of sheep hunters into their mountain camps along with their guides and all the gear, I have been so 'bushed' by nightfall that crawling into bed was a chore." If the truth be known, that's closer to it than anything you may see or hear glamorized to the contrary. It is just plain hard work.

Alaskan pilots? Are they the best in the world? Don't bet on it. The world is filled with very skilled pilots but for some reason, it is here that they get glamorized. Take for instance the high country around Salmon, Idaho with its hot, dry mountain air. Or the jungles of South America with just the opposite in wet, humid conditions. Wyoming, with its 7000 foot high airports on hot, dusty days, where some airplanes can not even get off the ground, is another example. Or the icing conditions so prevalent in the crowded south-eastern states — are these pilots any less because they don't happen to fly in Alaska? I think not.

What does seem to happen in the bush, especially with young pilots, is they are exposed very early in their careers to flying that looks deceptively easy from the passenger's seat. And since many of these future aviators are up here in Alaska as much for the outback and the freedom it entails, it is only natural for them to want to duplicate what they see being done with clockwork regularity when they start flying themselves.

But, even the most experienced of flyers get into trouble at times. In my own case, I've gotten out of the airplane and puked my guts out or had my knees so rubbery and shaking that had anyone seen me then, I would have been asked to have taken an evaluation test for my sanity. Are we crazy to do that kind of flying? No more so than the free rock climbers whose passion is the rage currently sweeping the nation. I couldn't do that on a bet and probably wouldn't even if I could, but I certainly admire those who have the courage and confidence to reach for a single fingerhold expecting to succeed. Perhaps it's the being on the edge that counts. Can I get down on that little sand bar over there? Well....maybe.

When I first flew to Alaska in the helicopter and then returned to the States, a mechanic friend who had watched with interest my daily lessons and then saw me floundering off to actually work a chopper on the slope, very wisely brought me back down to earth when I returned.

"W-e-l-l," he dragged on with a mischievous grin all over his face, "so you're one of those famous Alaskan pilots I keep hearing so much about?" I knew what he was driving at and still thank him for setting me straight when it could have been so easy to let it all go to my head. I'd been to the big country that lures men still and had survived somehow, but it did not impress my friend. As far as he was concerned then, I was inexperienced. As far as I am concerned now, I am still inexperienced, relatively speaking. Every landing in an untried area is still a frontier and not to be taken lightly. Of course, a person's experience grows and you build on what you have behind you. Only the foolish would go at it otherwise.

Kirk Armstrong, Dick Armstrong's son, once told me about the marginal weather flying that Armstrong Air Service did with regularity from Dillingham, where some summers horizontal rain seemed to be the only choice they had. "Ted, it looks like we are flying in impossible conditions, and to you they probably would be. But you must remember we did not start with the impossible. We fly the same routes hundreds and even thousands of times. Occasionally we get caught in some marginal stuff we have to deal with because usually we are in the air when it happens. The next time that same situation arises, we know what worked the last time and so push on. Pretty soon that same situation becomes more or less routine and most of us no longer consider it marginal.

"Then something else is added along the way and now it's marginal again. We work around that as well and eventually, a doubly marginal situation becomes S.O.P. It looks impossible from the outside but we have worked into it slowly and know our limitations."

Another friend came up from Tennessee and went to work flying for Yute Air some years back. He was given his check ride by Phil Bingman, the owner and perhaps one of the best in the business of operating in marginal conditions. Phil didn't waste any time showing him the "low altitude, scud running" route between Dillingham and Togiak. Flying like that was a common occurrence in that area and a necessary obstacle to overcome if a business was to succeed. Phil Bingman knew how to succeed.

My friend flew me through that area years later. "See that bush over there," he pointed to a particular patch of willows that hung on the hillside. I noted we were flying well below all the hillsides in the area. "As you pass that, you turn left to 220 degrees and count seven seconds and you should see a big rock. There it is — see." The rock passed below us as he spoke.

"Now turn gently back to 270 and continue on. That maneuver will get you lined up positively on the valley ahead so you'll miss the hillsides we just passed, which have a habit of becoming shrouded in fog when you need it least. Now, see that bump of a hill coming up? If the clouds are touching that, you can't get over the pass around the next corner, so you make your turn out of here around behind the hump to the left. The valley falls away enough so there is room to turn if there is crud hanging in here as well. If there is clearance over the hump, then you can skim across the pass and from there, everything is down hill to Togiak."

My head was spinning as much as my friend's must have been at the time, but he made notes on that route and a dozen others as well. In good weather and during slow times, all the pilots ran the "low routes" until they felt their timing was right on. It paid off because in the six or seven years my friend flew for Yute, he used it often. It was rare for any of them not to be able to make it to Togiak with a paying load.

But once, in a fully loaded Cherokee, right before he got to Togiak, fog closed down on him and forced him to skim the alder brush. In trying to make a turn back to safety, the horizon faded to grey. In another second, he would have been flying totally blind in an area that has killed its share of daredevils. Without hesitating, he chopped the power and pushed the heavy Piper down into the hillside alders. The right wing caught and sheared instantly, spinning them around and sending them backwards into the brush. The plane came to a stop precariously pointed down the mountain, but it held and fortunately hadn't caught on fire. My friend's nose was broken but his was the only injury of the seven souls on board. The only "cargo" they were carrying was a five-gallon can of kerosene that someone had ordered in Togiak which was being delivered along with the passengers. The fire it provided brightened the long night, but when the rain started, they were forced to climb back into the wreckage and sit on forward tilting seats until dawn. There was little sleep, but they were all alive, thanks to my friend's quick action.

We toured the area in *Baldy Bird* once, and it indeed has more than its share of aircraft carcasses, testimony to those who were not so fortunate.

Weather is not the only marginal condition that a new pilot has to face. There is loading. What you got off the ground with yesterday you may or may not make it into the air with today. Just how heavy is all that gear you keep stuffing into the backseat of the Cub on that mountainside strip? Boned-out sheep meat adds up in a hurry and for sure, moose quarters are not all equal. Then there are the horns to tie on the struts and the hunter and the guide to worry about. Darkness is approaching and........

But I'm getting ahead of myself. This is the kind of flying that gets you so "bushed" it's hard to crawl into bed at night — if in fact you are even near somewhere there is a bed.

I never set out to work for a big game guide in Alaska, but when you are willing to work at anything — *anything* is possible. What I did set out to do was go on a wilderness pack-horse trip. Every time I saw a photograph of a string of horses being led up into the mountains, their packs all in place, with the wrangler out front in his everpresent cowboy hat, or read an article of such adventures, I imagined that to be one of the finest wilderness experiences possible. *The high country.* Just the sound of those words brought out feelings deep inside me that couldn't be denied forever.

Usually, these expeditions were depicted somewhere in the Rocky Mountains or in Canada. There was high country in Alaska, too, but for whatever reasons, I never seemed to get there because of being preoccupied chasing too many other things. Already, I had been in Alaska three years since my divorce and had a lot of free time on my hands in the fall and winters. Late one August (that's fall in Alaska), I had flown up to Nome after fishing season to see some of the gold country I'd heard so much about. There I met a couple of guys who were about to head out for their winter caribou meat supply.

Would I care to go along?

"Would I!" The gold, which had sat in the ground a few zillion years already, could wait another year.

And so in two Super Cubs, four of us departed Nome with enough gear and equipment to fill three and headed for the Kobuk River east of Kotzebue — one hundred and twenty miles east to be exact, and over three hundred and fifty miles from Nome. This was only the third or fourth time I'd gotten above the Arctic Circle since coming to Alaska, but once you've been there, something strange is always pulling you back. The land seems always so desolate and yet the attraction is there.

Along the Kobuk River, trees seem strangely out of place, but they add a dimension to a land already so beautiful that it gets a hold of you and keeps you dreaming always of returning. Our camp was at a major caribou crossing, where we sat and waited for the animals to swim the river and then climb out on the gravel bar in front of us, shaking themselves dry as they clicked their hooves practically into our camp. It was not hunting, but it did revive a part of me that had gone dormant. It also gave me my first taste of what it was like to be the pilot on a hunt.

Even after the work of butchering and loading, it took over an hour and thirty minutes in *Baldy Bird* to get to the freezer in Kotzebue. Another hour and a half to return while my partner lounged around the campfire and drank coffee the whole while.

"Ted, maybe I should head into town, also, and go back to work tomorrow. I could just make that evening flight to Nome if we left now."

More loading and packing and another three hours shot before I, too, got a chance to relax and enjoy the wilderness. The fact that my partner was helping with the gas bills sounded good at first, but that dimmed considerably as I crawled my numbed bones into my sleeping bag that night. At this time of year in Alaska and especially in the Arctic, the days are longer than anyone has the energy to see to completion.

But a lot came out of that chance meeting which took me above the Arctic Circle once more. We repeated the trip the following year and when the caribou were late in their migration, we set out looking for them and ended up on the Noatak River some miles west of the Gates of the Arctic National Park, which was even more splendid than our camp of the year before but without the trees. This definitely was the "land of little sticks." A goose hunt ensued, as well as a search for the fossilized ivory that washes out from the eroding banks along the desolate coast lines of the Chukchi Sea. Wooly mammoths and mastodons once roamed this land as the musk oxen still do, and to find a piece of something that walked where we now stood more than ten thousand years before made our flash on this earth even less significant. Soaking in the hot springs at Serpentine became a favorite stopover and the friendships grew, but I still hadn't gone on a pack-horse trip.

It was the spring that I returned from spending three months at sea where I had more than ample time to think about all the things I yet wanted to do in my life. First, I made a list of all the guides in Alaska who used horses and then made a second list of all the guides who were kind to their horses. My plan was to volunteer to do anything that might need doing around a hunting camp. Chop wood, carry water, cook, or do whatever. As long as I would get to go on a pack-horse trip up into the high country, I didn't care what I'd have to do. Of course, I could have paid someone to take me up in the hills on horses but for me, that wasn't any challenge. Some things you can't really buy.

In the process of doing all this, a pilot friend told me of a guide he knew looking for help. He had the horses, and as far as he knew, treated them somewhat humanely. At least he fed them hay all winter rather than turn them out in some remote valley to fend for themselves along with the moose and the wolves. I called and told him what I had in mind. He seemed more interested in discussing the belly tank that I'd just acquired for my Cub than talking about horses.

"Ever haul fuel in that thing?"

"That's what it's for. I hope to be able to supply my gold mine someday, and it sure helps out when I'm roaming around the *tullies*. The mention of gold put us in the same groove almost at once and he asked me to meet him for lunch the next day.

Although, he had a pilot lined up for the following season, there was the possibility of me hauling fuel into his remote camps with my belly tank. After I got my assistant guide's license, he would get me out on a pack-horse trip. I had to have thirty days in the field and his recommendation to get the license but at least I would be in the mountains.

"Ever hunt sheep or moose?"

"No, but I have hunted caribou in the Arctic and white tails in Pennsylvania." He was from Ohio, my neighboring home state, and so another harmonizing cord was struck between us. We agreed to meet on the Tonsina air strip August 4th. I'd have to waste no time in closing up my fishing operation, then fly the four hundred miles from Dillingham to Palmer, pick up my hunting gear, and then fly another nearly two hundred miles to Tonsina. He would have liked me to come even earlier since sheep season opens the tenth of August, but it was the best I could do. His other pilot would handle everything until then.

Two and a half months later, I was taking a nap in the beautiful warm sunshine along Tonsina's grass strip when he drove in. He didn't fly himself and his good-looking yellow and black Super Cub was tied down on the field along with my *Baldy Bird*. I thought it strange, this being his busiest time of year, that his airplane was sitting idle like that, but I said nothing. We made our greetings and chatted a while. I met his wife and two-year-old daughter and even heard a few of his stories before he got around to the reason his airplane was sitting idle.

His pilot had busted off the landing gear a week before at his main camp, and they decided he should head on down the road. The Cub had just gotten out of the repair shop, and he was still without a pilot. "How'd you like to do all the flying for us?" he asks, then adds, "Sure would get us out of a bind."

I had been nervous already about hauling the fuel, let alone his clients and guides and all the other materials that would be required to keep a remote hunting lodge operating in the mountains. I had very little mountain flying experience other than the caribou hunting up near the Brooks Range and told him so.

"I'd need some serious practice before I'd feel even remotely comfortable, and then I couldn't guarantee anything," I answered, the vision of my long-awaited pack-horse trip slipping away as I spoke.

"Take the Cub and practice all you want. I can charter everything in for a few days with the float-equipped Beaver up the road, and we can pack it the two miles to camp on the horses from there to get things rolling." He was more than accommodating as we discussed how to handle the two airplanes. Mine would be left at the camp and used only in the event his was damaged somehow.

After I got a roughly sketched map of where the camp was in relation to the mountains that surrounded Tonsina, I tossed my sleeping roll into his airplane and headed out. As I climbed up out of that hole at the base of the mountains, I realized the Wrangells were on one side of the strip and the Chugach on the other. The power lines at the end of the runway came all too close and I wondered if maybe I was biting off a bit too much as I turned north and headed for Snowshoe Lake and the Oddens, folks I knew from Wisconsin. Jim and Mary had a Cub, too, and had lived in the area a long time. I was counting on them to point me to someone who could show me what I needed to know about working an airplane in the mountains.

Gracious as always, they welcomed me into their home and listened to what I'd gotten myself into. "Let's take him over to meet Lloyd Ronning," Mary was saying. "He's been flying a Cub in these mountains for twenty years and if anybody knows anything about it, he does," Jim added. "But he may not talk to you. He's been known to tip the bottle now and then so he may not be in the mood."

Lloyd was busy with a neighbor in his garage putting the finishing touches to a new fabric job on his Cub when we walked in. The timing was wrong so after introductions and some talk about the remarkable weather we were having, we excused ourselves and I ended up back at the Odden's cabin for the night. It was as apparent to them as it was to me that I was nervous about this whole venture. Jim and I sat up talking long into the night to help ease my tensions.

The next morning, Jim and Mary loaned me the use of their old Blazer and told me to make myself at home as they rushed off to work in Glennallen some forty miles away. I was left alone in their beautiful eight-sided log cabin with its picture windows overlooking the sun-drenched, glacier-filled Chugach Mountains to the south. Sitting there by myself, I wondered if maybe Mr. Ronning would feel more comfortable talking if I approached him alone, so I tried again.

This time, after I explained what was going on and that I was afraid I'd bitten off more than I could handle, he mellowed right out. For the next several hours, I got a more thorough schooling in mountain flying than any university could have provided. Pencil and paper diagrams, rules, do's and don'ts, and otherwise were all covered. The gist of the whole thing was that mountain flying was not to be underestimated in any way at any time. Those who had were no longer here to tell about it.

"Go up here to the store and buy yourself a bag of flour," Ronning said. "And then go over to the little airport across the road and mark off a section three hundred feet long. When you can get down and stopped and back off again in that distance, then you go into the mountains. And remember what I said about the cross wind and keeping your load centered and tying on horns or whatever and don't be afraid to back down if things don't look right."

He reached out and put a hand on my shoulder as I was leaving. My confidence needed all the bolstering it could get. Then he added, "You'll do fine, but be careful!" It was that same piece of advice, a standard in aviation circles, that was coming back to me once again; I fully intended to make use of it.

Getting down and stopped in three hundred feet? Could he be serious, I thought, as the first floured line went zipping under the wheels? The pair of white lines down on the runway had looked like a pedestrian crossing at a large intersection of a busy city on my first try, but I remembered what Lloyd had said.

"You have to be able to hit the first line exactly on the spot at touchdown because if you're ten feet past, you're likely to be ten feet into the rocks and brush at the other end of the strip when you get into the mountains. If you're short, it will likely be just as bad or worse. There is no excuse for landing short — any time."

And so I began and by late that afternoon could hit the first mark usually within a foot or two, but I could not get it slowed down and stopped before the second one went sliding under me. Sometimes only fifty feet over but usually more. I could do everything he said easily in four hundred feet but I knew I was being cautious with the big 29 inch tundra tires under me. I'd heard plenty of stories of guys who had gone over on their noses when over-braking, and I didn't intend to wreck an airplane before I actually started.

Another night with the Oddens. The next morning they dropped me off on their way to work at the little strip where they kept *Rags*, the Cub they had flown extensively between Wisconsin, Montana, and Dahl Creek until they moved here to Snowshoe Lake. It was the same strip I'd used to practice what Lloyd had told me the morning before. After our goodbyes, it was time for me to head into the unknown once again.

"Come back any time you need a break, Ted," Jim hollered as they drove off. "You're always welcome. You know that!"

I got out the roughly sketched map and headed to the camp at Manker Creek. In route, I decided to try out another strip close to Tonsina Lake which was on the map as well. It was supposedly seven hundred feet long at an elevation of two thousand feet, and would be a good place to get started in this business of mountain flying before going into the main camp. The airstrip at the main camp was pushing three thousand in elevation and, although listed at seven hundred feet long, had a dog leg at one end, making it considerably shorter for all practical purposes.

The wind was pouring off the glacier and down the lake when I arrived. I'd have to land down hill towards the water, and now wished I hadn't used the term "get my feet wet" in my thinking when I decided to make this my first mountain landing. After a couple of slow passes, there was nothing left to do but take the chance and land. All the practice in the world still leaves you with an empty feeling in your stomach when it comes time to put down in a strange place the first time. Again, my throat was dry when I tried to swallow as I set up the approach and placed my two imaginary flour lines across the strip. Technically all you had to do then was fly the line from where you were to the line on the ground as slowly as conditions allowed. It took me better than five hundred feet to get stopped, but at least I didn't have wet feet.

There was much to do and even more to learn in those first few weeks. The spike camps, Upper Manker, Maylo, Black Mountain, Klutina, Grayling, Upper and Lower Tonsina, all became familiar both as to the animals that were found there and the characteristics of the strips involved. Some were one way in and then out in opposite directions, regardless of the wind. I was glad I'd spent the time with Mr. Ronning. Elevations varied, too. 4300 feet was our highest but once I landed, fully loaded, on the side of a mountain at 5900 feet among the rocks and gravel. It was one of those lessons I learned but was glad it hadn't cost the outfitter his airplane. I never tried it again.

I learned, too, about the guides and guiding. Most I hit it off with right away, but there were some more willing to teach me than others, and I found myself gravitating towards them at every opportunity. All were younger than I, and it was tough keeping up with them sometimes. As I got to know them better the old joke about "old age and treachery will always overcome youth

and skill" became the byword and everyone started using it on anyone who was younger than himself, and we laughed and joked continuously.

After particularly successful hunts, we all would usually find ourselves sitting around an evening bonfire (weather permitting) participating in a sing-a-long with the banjo and guitar players in camp. Everyone would always be in high spirits and the stories would be snapping and bouncing around as much as the sparks from spruce logs on the fire. Our outfitter was, by far, the best storyteller any of us had ever come across. It was nearly impossible to tell if it was B.S. or not, but it didn't matter. He could hold hunters and assistant guides spellbound for long intervals with his tales. It gave me a good feeling just to be there and to know that I had a part in the whole thing.

The hunts and stories rolled by. As one group prepared to leave, names and addresses were usually exchanged with invitations to come visit any time we were in the lower 48. We almost always became like family during these ten-day to two-week intervals. Then another group would be there and the cycle would repeat itself with new friendships blossoming all over again.

Before I knew it, snow had come and the season ended. I volunteered to stay on a couple of months to watch the camp while the regular winter couple went back home to Michigan to get married.

In the spring, the whole operation was moved down to Kodiak Island to hunt the big brown bears. It was the first time they had taken an airplane along, and I got the dubious honor of flying it down there over the sixty miles of open water — on wheels no less! Kodiak has weather on top of weather to contend with and beaches that are even more dangerous on which to land, but the season went well, and I got to be a part of several hunts for the big bears so my experience continued to grow.

I couldn't wait for my fishing season to end that summer so I could get back to the mountains and the "yellow cub" once again. The guide had expanded his hunting area and another pilot and airplane were added to the staff. All of a sudden, I was the old-timer in camp. At forty-seven, I was in fact older but didn't feel the title justified just because I had flown there longer than the new fellow who brought plenty of experience with him as well.

But, with another airplane around, I was finally free enough to go on my long awaited pack-horse trip. Since I had already flown over the entire area many times and had even hiked up into the high country that I had dreamed about so much, it was not all that I had expected it to be when we finally got there on horseback. Horses have minds of their own, and it was obvious we did not speak the same language. They had guts though, climbing up hills that would burst a man's heart had we been able to endure what they did with the same regularity.

Once, after a particularly hard day on a moose hunt, I felt sorry for the easy-gaited small black gelding that had carried me so effortlessly around the hills and swamps that we had hunted. The horses were hobbled for the night and turned out to graze after they had their ration of grain, except one which was kept tied up so someone could go out in the morning and round up the others if the rattle of the grain buckets didn't bring them painfully hobbling into camp. But that small black had burned a hole in my heart, and so I took its hobbles off and set it free, thinking it could get at the choicest grasses as a special reward for its efforts.

Our wrangler had once told me, "Ted, this is not the wild west of movie land and these horses are not your friends."

That #*%&*#! little black led the whole string thirteen miles back the trail to main camp. All were hobbled and lathered white with sweat except the innocent little black. It was a mess for a while, but when I finally got back to camp, I was determined to have a talk with a certain little black gelding, even if we didn't speak the same language.

I found it in the corral along with the others, but every time I tried to get a hand on its halter, it jerked its head and walked away. "OK," I said aloud. "You want to play games? We will play games but you are going to let me get a hand on you and you are not getting out until you do."

The halter-catching competition intensified until finally I was lunging at the halter, but always the black's head would be inches out of reach as it spun around and trotted to the opposite side of the log corral. By now, I was darting after it and just as quickly, it would dart the other way. Finally, in a desperate leap, I lost my footing and landed flat out face down in horse manure and mud that oozed up between my fingers. As I slowly pushed myself up, I tried not to notice the guide's wife giggling at the gate where she had come to take her own bay for a ride and had watched the whole show.

My "horse sense" grew more slowly than anything I'd ever tried and the pun was intended. In main camp, the first job of the day was usually to get the horses back to the corral. Because this was "home" to them, hobbles were never used and the rattle of the grain bucket and a whistle usually brought them on a trot because eating brush was obviously not as appealing as the oats they very quickly learned to relish. Put down some pans of grain amongst a group of horses, and you will learn almost immediately that chickens do not have the franchise on pecking order. Horses can be violent to each other and you wouldn't want to get between two who hadn't settled things yet. They also had the uncanny ability to know which mornings they would be saddled up and loaded down with camping gear to be ridden away from their beloved grain supply. On these mornings, the airplane would be put into service to locate the "critters" who were usually in the thickest alders and spruce they could find while one of the assistant guides would be dispatched with the grain bucket in the direction my tight circling and dives indicated.

I would be waiting by the corral and hitching posts, where I had already rationed out the correct number of grain piles, when the beasts and the searcher came sauntering in. One particular day, one of the pack horses arrived without its halter so I went to the equipment shed and got another, thinking I would slip it on while it was eating its pile of oats. Wrong. Every time I went near, its head went flying and it pushed or kicked its way to the grain ration of one of the lesser animals until very soon it was near bedlam around the hitching posts while this game of musical oats was inflicted on the whole lot. But once started, I figured that no horse was going to get the best of me, so I intensified my part and made sure that that pack horse, no matter how dominant it was towards the others, was not going to taste another drop of oats until the halter was in place.

"First you get the halter—then you get the grain," I stated in no uncertain terms as it bolted away once again. After about fifteen minutes of this, it took a few steps away and looked back to where I was standing by the nearest pile of grain, still holding out the halter. We may not have spoken the same language, but the message got through. Unfortunately, it wasn't me doing the shouting any more. Calmly, as though nothing at all had been going on, it reached over to the nearest bush and grabbed a mouthful of limbs, tearing the wood off in one powerful thrust of its neck. And looking back at me once more, quietly stepped off into the brush, choosing to eat sticks rather than letting me have the last say.

And so my "horse days" were not what I had anticipated. I admired them at times and hated them at others. But...I was glad I had the Yellow Bird to depend on. We, at least, did speak the same language.

By the third season, our area was once more expanded to the point where we had two "Main Camps" a hundred miles apart. The boss stayed at the new headquarters while I stayed out in my old familiar territory. Now I was the old man in camp even though the next new pilot, who stayed with the boss, had the time and experience to put me in his hip pocket. Whenever either of us got too busy, we would join forces, thanks to the short wave radio that connected the two outposts.

It was this newcomer with all his experience who led me into my first glacier landing on solid ice at 4200 feet. Scary as heck but a lot easier when you get to fly circles overhead while watching and listening as the pro talked me through the procedure. The trick was to hit the touchdown area exactly, as the only smooth ice to be found was only a couple hundred feet long on the entire glacier. The trouble was that the only way to identify the area from the air was from the huge boulders which had come crashing down from the nearly vertical canyon walls that hemmed in the lower end of the valley where the ice was squeezing through. To further compound the situation, you had to land uphill under full power over the boulders where the surrounding terrain rose around you more rapidly than the Cub could climb. Simply put, this was a totally committed landing. There would be no all-saving "go around" here.

Once on the glacier and slowed down, you had to steer around the roughest spots and then taxi a quarter-mile up hill through the rivulets of melting water to get to the camp that had previously been established.

The Iowa hunter I took in with me that first time sat spellbound at the awesomeness of where we were going as we circled through the 6,000 foot peaks, watching the old pro below us as he touched down amid a showering of ice crystals and water, his big Borer prop at full power as he dragged the little Cub up the ice.

"Man," he said, "I can't believe you guys fly into places like this."

"Me, neither. In fact, I've never even been here before," I answered as I made the final turn to set up our approach. The words were out before I realized what I'd said. The silence from the rear seat filled the cockpit but there was no time for any reassurances on my part—we were committed.

The more you fly in the bush, the more normal the not-so-normal becomes. Once I'd taken one trip too many when darkness was approaching to get a guy moved into a bear camp. He was a big fellow and weight was a consideration, but when I was leaving to go make the switch, something told me to dump an extra five gallons of gas into the Cub. Hunches were to be followed, I was learning in my life. They were not all relevant, but this one saved my butt.

I moved the guide in first to our bear hole on the Klutina River and then went back for the hunter. I knew it would be close but now felt committed. When the hunter was unloaded, his guide looked to the dwindling light in the west and asked, "You gonna' make it alright? You can stay here, you know."

"I think I'll be OK," I answered as I crawled in and fired up the Cub once more.

When I got to Manker Creek, I regretted I hadn't taken him up on the offer. The valley was dark, the short gravel strip with the dog-leg barely visible in the last light of the day. I made one pass and then another but whenever I got down low, everything went black and I couldn't make out the touch down spot.

Soon, I saw the flickering of flashlights running out to the strip from the lodge. In another few minutes they had fires burning at each side of the runway where I was to touch down, and a couple more at what I hoped was the halfway mark to give me some directional control. This was the plan we had discussed in the event such an emergency ever came about and it was here! Unfortunately, this was our first practice run and here I was making the approach to four camp fires in the black of night and I thought flour marks on the runway were hard to hit!

Just as I was about to touch down, the two nearest flames turned into giant fireballs, blinding me of everything I'd focused on. Someone had thrown gasoline on the fires at that moment, thinking it would help me see the runway. There was nothing I could do but cram the throttle full forward and head back up into the black of night. I made a circle, waved the wing tip navigation lights, and headed for the highway at Tonsina. It was a long twenty-five minute ride with the gauges bouncing on empty the whole way. I was grateful for the extra five gallons my hunch had given me, but my problems were far from over. I knew the wires across the unlighted runway in Tonsina would be waiting for me, but at least I had eighteen hundred feet to play with instead of the five hundred at camp, and I made it fine. No one in the Mangy Moose Saloon believed that I had just landed there in the dark, but then they hadn't been with me the last hour either.

Eventually, with a little experimenting, we worked out a landing light system at Manker Creek and even the two gals who did the cooking were instructed on how to carry it out, because they were often the only ones left in camp when all the hunters were in the field. Three flashlights, small fires, anything—just so they didn't blind me was all that was needed. The rule now was to walk out to the middle of the strip, face the wind, and then place a single light in the center of the runway. Then turn around, walk to the touchdown area, and place the remaining two lights on each side of the strip. That way, from the air, I would be looking at a triangle of sorts with the long point going into the wind.

The possibility that I might be pressing it a bit finally got drummed into my head towards the middle of that third season. I was wandering back to camp through the canyons after a particularly stressful day, or maybe it was a week. The boss was at the other headquarters, and I had some hunters down on me because of a problem with one of the guides. I was the direct link with the boss because of the airplane. Every night there seemed to be something new that needed to be resolved, and it always happened in my tent. It was going to be several more days before the boss could get out our way and straighten out the mess, and I was stuck in the middle. All of a sudden, this whole pack-horse adventure wasn't fun any more.

Thoughts were racing through my head. The closer I got to Manker, the more I dreaded another confrontation with the unhappy clients. I was completely preoccupied with the situation—until something caught my attention outside. The valley was coming up under me at an alarming rate. I had flown into a dead-end canyon without thinking! The wheels were scraping the willows by the time I got turned around and my knees were rubbery. When I got back to my tent, I wrote out my resignation while the shaking was still going on inside me. I had to get away from the most fun thing I had ever done in my life. A cloud shadowed the dream that had drawn me here. The life forces within me were making themselves known once more, and I had no choice but to go where they pointed. Already, I had come further than I ever thought possible since that day I spread those first flour marks under Lloyd Ronning's advice. And now I remembered too that he said, "Don't be afraid to back away from any situation that doesn't feel right." I've never looked back.

chapter 11

We are reluctant to leave the protection of the tent for any reason, as the screened doorway is alive with insects. Mosquitoes and whitesox are everywhere and the hum soon fills our ears. It would be easy to go mad out here on this mountainside without some kind of protection, and I am glad the survival gear that *Baldy Bird* has carried for nearly ten years was intact.

Later, when we are outside, we are still "inside" our head nets. It is a brilliant day overhead, without a breath of wind, but all around us the clouds hang low and menacing near the mountains. No one will come looking for us this day either. Once again we find ourselves surveying the crash sight for what could easily be the "ten millionth" time since our accident almost a week ago. Whitney says jokingly that we should dig for gold where *Baldy Bird* first hit the ground. It is not such a bad idea. Gold had been discovered in these mountains long before the dream of men flying here had become a reality. As close as we can figure, we are less than ten miles from the old hydraulic gold mine at Canyon Creek which had operated off and on since 1902.

Always, it has remained a mystery to me how those early prospectors managed. With little more than determination, they scoured the western states, much of Canada and apparently all of Alaska. What was even more astounding was to hike into some remote valley somewhere with all your belongings in your pack — barely able to negotiate the rugged terrain underfoot — only to find someone had already been there. Not only had been there, but had gotten huge steel pipes, steam engines, and tons of other equipment there as well. The rusty remains scattered throughout the landscape, a dim reminder of days gone by, boggled the imagination. Men certainly were tough in those early years, but maybe they were desperate, too.

We were desperate for only one thing and that was another bath. Two things were necessary before either of us dared plunge into the frigid water of the stream that had been sustaining us since our food ran out: Sunshine and wind. Actually, we had had enough wind the other night to last us both a lifetime. It was a breeze we needed to keep the confounded bugs at bay; and we needed the warmth of the sun to dry our bodies afterward. The exhilaration and well-being we felt after a dunking was beyond description. Looking back, I wish we had built a sweat lodge with the tent fly and hot rocks but we still would have needed the sun and breeze to survive the insects and the cold plunge afterwards.

As we wound our way down off the mountain towards the river along what had become "our trail," it was hard not to think of the gold and the men that had been lured to these mountains to fight the ancestors of these same critters that plagued us now. Even desperate men would have been hard pressed here without some protection. Whitney and I had already managed a couple of baths when the conditions had presented themselves. There had not been much notice. We were boiling some blueberry tea down by the river and trying to keep the smoke of the fire out of our eyes when the sun burst through the clouds that first time. Its warmth overshadowed the pleasantness of the fire while the gurgling stream took precedence. We were out of our clothes in a flash and into the water and back by the fire almost as instantly because the sun disappeared once more behind the clouds. Still, we felt renewed somehow and never missed an opportunity after that. The river had drawn us to it right from the start. We drank it, we fished in it, we bathed in it and we wondered about the gold in it. Easy to do when there seemed to be only two of us on earth. Add a few million bodies downstream and the problems of the world become apparent at once. Open another hydraulic mine like the one up at Canyon Creek, and you would have the wrath of the Sierra Club, The Friends of the Earth, and Greenpeace on you all at once. Still, the thought of having a gold mine someday stayed with me, and Whitney and I talked about it at great length. It certainly was a conflict of interest.

* * * * *

I used to think fishermen were close-mouthed until I met my first gold prospector. When I saw his small vial of nuggets, I couldn't hold back. "Where'd you get those?" I exclaimed as I rolled the vial around to look at the various shapes.

"In Alaska."

"I know that," I answered, still not aware of what was going on. "But where?"

"Just Alaska," he answered again. The conversation ended every time the subject of where came up. How, when, what, who were all valid questions, but nothing about where.

In the prospecting class I took through the University of Alaska, we were discussing "chimneys," a particular rock formation associated with diamonds which at that time had not yet been discovered in the state. The instructor was showing us a slide of one such typical formation with a helicopter perched nearby and a majestic glacier in the background.

Someone in the class asked, "What's the name of that glacier in the background?" Instantly, the slide went off the screen.

"Sorry," he answered, and we went on to something else. Ask a prospector anything, but don't ask where.

Gold stories have always fascinated me. I enjoyed Jack London's accounts long before I ever got to Alaska, but when I got here myself, nothing stirred my blood more than talking with someone who had first-hand information about gold, even if that information was a generation or two old.

Ken's dad had told him stories of the sheep hunter who had been dumped off with an airplane in the Brooks Range for a ten-day hunt. He had been glassing a distant mountain when something shiny caught his attention. It took considerable effort to reach the spot, but when the sheep hunter did, he couldn't believe his eyes — a vein of gold was exposed in the rocks. He was rich! To get samples, he ended up using all of his ammunition to knock a chunk loose and then had to wait eight days without bear protection or the chance to shoot his sheep, until his plane returned to the pre-designated pick-up point some miles away. He needed to get back to civilization where he could get organized to come back and stake the area properly and to get the legal paperwork in order. Winter set in before he could get back, but he returned the following summer, having dreamed and planned all the while what he was going to do with his wealth. The gold vein was gone. Had he somehow missed the spot? Had the mountain covered it over once more in a landslide or a winter avalanche changed the area somehow? The sheep hunter died of old age still searching and wondering.

Another fellow I heard about had a similar experience when he stumbled across a small stream out in the tundra somewhere and found a shallow pool where the bottom was yellow. He supposedly filled his pockets and marked the area very carefully. He too had to walk away from there to meet his pick-up airplane and to this day has not been able to relocate the spot.

Gold does funny things to men and stories like that have kept me on edge since I first found my way north so many years ago. They are the makings of the rainbows we have been titillated with since our nursery rhyme days. Gold and rainbows go together somehow, but it doesn't really matter. I knew I was hung up on gold ever since I found that first flake on Caribou Creek the year I bought *Baldy Bird*. In the dozen years since, I've very systematically set about learning everything I could about gold and prospecting and mining to eventually come to the very conclusion that all men seem to come to eventually. That it's not the gold we're wanting, but the search that counts. (To paraphrase a bit of Robert Service's *The Spell of the Yukon*.)

Gold does not come easy to anyone regardless of the stories one hears. My own experience has more

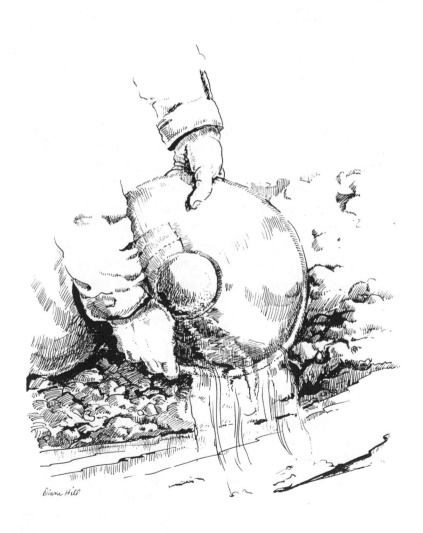

Diane Hill

memories of sweat, and aching backs, and knees that refuse to straighten out after a long session of panning than of any glitter in the pan.

Oh, once another friend and I did manage to suck up an ounce and a half in two hours with a small back-pack dredge we lugged into a remote area. But our bonanza was short-lived. The pay streak seemed to vaporize while the sweat on our brows continued to remind us of the miles and miles we still had to go to get out of there.

Another time, I had hiked up a valley in a slogging rain decked out in a hooded rain jacket and hip waders carrying my shovel and pans. I was nearly exhausted by the time I got to the area I wanted to examine and sweat had me nearly as wet on the inside as I would have been had I been naked in the rain, but there was no relief. As soon as the rain stopped, the mosquitoes came out with a vengeance that made me wish for more rain. My head net came out from a pocket instead. And so I settled down to work along the stream bank as the maddening clouds of critters thumped against the netting only inches from my face and relentlessly attacked my hands which was the only exposed skin on my body. I filled the grizzly with gravel as quickly as possible and got down into the water to wash it into the pan. I relished the chilling wetness as the stream soothed the itching agony on the backs of my hands, but later, as I was swirling the pan beneath the cooling surface, a dozen mosquitoes (by actual count) were firmly sticking their thirsting snouts into each thumb that remained above the water line. I never did finish the pan.

Yet, I know deep inside me that I could spend the rest of my life chasing down and listening to other men's tales of the gold that waits for them "just over the horizon." It doesn't matter where they lead, for I seem to follow wherever they go.

An ad caught my eye some years back. "Come to Nome and work in a real gold mine. One week, two weeks or all summer. Experience the thrill of finding your own gold." Of course there was a "fee" involved, but when you deal in gold, things seem to make sense where they probably wouldn't otherwise. So I paid my "fee" for a two-week stay and flew myself up to Nome at the end of fishing season.

One thing you learn quickly about gold ventures is scams. The alluded-to promises of many having more than paid for their stay at the mine with the gold they found were pipe dreams at best. Oh, sure — somebody probably did find some — once. What these paying miners did receive though, myself included, was a chance to relive a part of history. To come to Nome where gold is still king and it is still possible to take a shovel and a pan and go down to that same beach that once harbored twenty thousand glory-seeking miners (even if they were desperate) and do what they had done at the turn of the century was true adventure for us modern-day miners. Not much really changes with gold.

Later that winter, a fellow I had met at the mine in Nome called me from Houston.

"Want to go to Costa Rica and do the same thing we did in Nome?"

I started laughing because this was the very same guy who a few months prior had uncovered some very shaky scruples going on in our mining camp and had sworn he was going to expose the whole thing. That's the point of a good scam—there is usually enough right about it to make it believable and it's virtually impossible to uncover the wrongs. I had already heard about the mines in Costa Rica that were salted and then sold, and then worked and then re-salted and sold again. It had been going on for years.

"No, this will be different," he assured me. "Besides, as long as you keep your wallet in your pocket, how can you get into trouble?"

A month later, Bill and I each had paid our thousand dollars which was to include "all costs" and were on our way to the Phantom Isle Lodge somewhere in the jungles in southern Costa Rica. It would at least be a good winter break from the rigors of another Alaskan dark spell.

San Jose was beautiful but had more people than I was comfortable with. I wish I'd spoken some Spanish though, because the señoritas sure seemed to smile a lot at us big gringos. After spending a night in a hotel, the twelve of us were stuffed, bags and equipment included, into a nine-passenger Japanese van and headed south two hundred miles to a place known as Palmer. There, we were to board a small boat which would take us down a jungle river and out into the Pacific to a place called Drake's Bay, where we would find the Phantom Isle Lodge.

There was much confusion and many delays, but eventually we arrived in the middle of night, the tiny boat crammed with all our belongings and 24 single bed mattresses which had to be loaded at the last moment. I couldn't help rubbing it in to Bill when at last the boat bumped against a fallen-over tree that was used as the dock and we were led up the narrow jungle path carrying our own mattress. Phantom Isle

Lodge was a giant blue tarp strung between two palms. There would be no problem with my wallet staying put on this trip.

Being exposed to metal detectors in Costa Rica, I decided to take one back to Alaska where I'd heard of some terrific finds in some of the tailings piles from the old gold workings. These are the gravel piles that the early miners worked through and left behind in their wake. The best tailings piles were those left by the big dredges, especially the trummel types that had gone through an area where coarse gold had been found. All rock and gravel was washed in a tumbler which, due to its inherent design, had holes in its sides to let the gold pass through while the debris was dumped out behind the dredge. It was not uncommon to have chunks of gold too large to be filtered out with the tumbler to find their way out to the tailings piles where they have been waiting for years for someone, like myself, to come along and find them with a metal detector.

It seemed only natural to get some formal training in the use of a detector if I were going to go to all the trouble of getting back into the bush once I got to Alaska. Through a friend in California, I was introduced to Woody Woodward from nearby Course Gold on the edge of the Sierra's. Woody was a former government trapper, fly fisherman extraordinare, and Sierra tour guide. Unfortunately, the first two hours he had a metal detector in his hand, he stumbled across a thirteen ounce gold nugget which about ruined his life because he has spent every waking moment since then trying to do it over again.

We spent a week together out in the desert just north of the great Mohave salt flats where Woody had worked with his uncle in the gold mines as a young man more than 50 years before. That's where he stumbled across the big nugget. It was less than thirty feet from where they had quit digging nearly two generations ago and was only an inch below the surface. We found only a match-head sized nugget for our efforts, but I felt comfortable using both of the metal detectors I ended up buying from Woody.

Just before heading to Bristol Bay for another summer's fishing, I was having dinner with Ken Trowbridge. My metal detectors were safely tucked away in *Baldy Bird's* baggage compartment for the planned trip to Nome at season's end. My recent activities down in California came up in the conversation.

"I've got one of those things, too, but I don't know the first thing about using it." And so I gave him a quick lesson out in his driveway and departed for the summer.

That fall, I was barely back home when the telephone started ringing. It was Ken. "When are you coming over?" he asked rather excitedly after inquiring about my successes up in Nome.

"I just got home, but Nome was a disaster gold-wise. Why?"

"Come on over for dinner and I'll tell you."

Perhaps I don't really have it in me to be a miner. The metal detector experience I had outside of Nome taught me an interesting lesson about myself and this fascination I have with gold. When I finally did locate the perfect area, there were some things I hadn't counted on. The darned trout kept making dimples on the surface of the nearby stream and the sound of its gentle gurgling kept getting in under my headphones where I was supposed to be listening for the sound of the tiny electronic beep that would signal my great forthcoming wealth. Oh, I resisted temptation for the better part of two hours or so but the trout and the gurgling won out. My fly rod replaced the metal detector in my hands, and my ears no longer were hampered as the sounds of that wild place filled the depths of my being. The gold would have to wait a while longer for me to find it.

Ken was as nervous as a squirrel hiding in an attic. "You mean you didn't find anything?"

"Well, I did find a bucket-full of nuts and bolts and old nails and junk. Even a button off an old set of Helly Hansons but nothing that glittered."

"Boy, too bad," he said as he casually tossed a quarter sized nugget down on the table.

"Where did you get that?" In my excitement, the taboo question just slipped out.

"With that metal detector you showed me how to use." He ignored my *faux pas* and laid down another nugget even larger than the first. He had my full attention but couldn't resist the *coup de grace* as he casually unwrapped another he had folded up in a new handkerchief. It was an inch thick and four inches across. I was speechless.

The story was simple: Ken had met this miner shortly after I went fishing. He had this huge nugget that he had found in his sluice box, but it had a large chunk broken off from one corner. He was sure the missing piece was somewhere in the tailing pile at his mine. It took some talking but Ken finally convinced the miner that he could find the missing chip with his metal detector. Miners don't like strangers in their camps, but Ken is so personable and likeable that his promise not to reveal anything pertinent convinced even this grizzled veteran to make an exception this one time. It was a good move.

In the week that Ken was there he not only found the missing "chip" — all sixteen ounces of it, but he found another twenty-seven ounce chunk the miner had completely passed over and several other lesser pieces. In all, he found $200,000 worth. The $15,000 that I was looking at was Ken's reward from one very pleased miner. Ken never even hinted as to the location. But then, I didn't tell him where the trout were biting either.

That first winter I was on my own after my marriage ended I spent near Central at Arctic Circle Hot Springs. It is one of the biggest mining areas in the state, outside of Nome. There I had the opportunity to meet most of the miners in the area and even got to help in some clean-ups at season's end when they came in to utilize the warm water bubbling out of the springs long after snow and ice blanketed the area. It was really something to see the ounces and ounces of fine gold that came out of pan after pan of the black sand these men had been accumulating all summer. It came from the tons and tons of gravel they had pushed into their sluices with the D-9 Cats their operations required. I don't feel good around big machinery like that and the work it entails keeping it operating, but I sure enjoyed listening to their stories while we filtered through their summer's take.

It was there I met several couples who mined together as well. "Mom and Pop" kind of operations. One couple only worked their claims every other year while a third partner worked them on the alternate seasons. They spent their winters making jewelry from the gold they mined and then traveled to fairs and gold shows during their non-mining summers selling their wares. It seemed an almost idyllic life-style.

Tom and Twila live in Fairbanks. They too had mined together in years past but had finally drifted away from it into other pursuits. They were newlyweds sometime during the sixties and had practically nothing to start out with except each other and the use of a vacant cabin in an abandoned mining town. It seemed like it would be a good place to get to know each other and make plans for the family they someday hoped they could afford. Tom had always been attracted to gold mines and miners and had worked with a few already in his young life. He had heard the stories of the strange bachelor brothers who mined together for thirty years without speaking to each other for as long as anyone could remember. Eventually, one of the brothers died, and supposedly the survivor spent his remaining days searching for the gold he suspected his brother had cheated from him. All this had taken place during the depression years, yet their dilapidated cabin still stood as a reminder to those who had heard the stories.

Tom and Twila passed the cabin often on their walks out of the old ghost town and onto the tundra that surrounded the tiny, abandoned log settlement. They were in love, and it was grand to just be together and alone amidst all the splendor that surrounded them, but Tom felt something strange tugging at his chest every time they passed the bachelor's cabin on their walks.

"It went on all summer," Tom told me. "Each time I passed the cabin, the urge or whatever it was kept getting stronger. Something physical was drawing me to that place. It was weird but I kept it to myself."

Finally, toward the end of summer, Twila had stayed behind this one day to take some bread out of the oven while Tom strolled amidst the abandoned cabins. This time, he let the urge prevail. As he neared the cabin, the tugging in his chest was stronger than ever before.

Outside the cabin door was a pile of junk and trash strewn about by countless curiosity seekers as they rummaged through the now long-dead bachelor's belongings. For years people had been sifting through things, hoping to find something of value. Tom, too, pawed about a bit and happened to kick at an old Crisco can. There was something about the "thud" that made him pick it up. It was different somehow and probably would have been too subtle for someone less tuned as he hefted the can in his hand. The lid was rusted fast and it took some searching among the debris to find a flat bar which Tom used to whack off the top of the can. Inside, an old greasy brown paper bag was where the white lard should have been. Inside that, was the leather pouch. Tom's hands were shaking as he tugged at the leather thongs to take his first peek inside. His screams brought Twila running with the 30/30 thinking her new husband was being mauled by a bear, and for a moment the little ghost town felt life once again much as it must have known so many years before. A little over two pounds of powdered yellow gold showed up out of the pouch.

That night they celebrated long and hard their good fortune, but were worried too. What about the family of the dead brothers? Did they still have a right to the gold no one knew about for sure but had wondered about for so long? They talked and talked long into the night.

At breakfast, the reality of what had happened finally dawned on Tom. "Miners always sell their fine gold first," he blurted out to Twila. "What happened to the nuggets?"

Systematically, they sifted through every scrap outside the cabin but found nothing. Inside, the mess was even worse. So, taking a two-foot swath around the outside wall, they started from the open door. Down one wall and around the corner, nothing was left unturned or unexamined. In the second corner, a pile of empty, half-rotten brown paper bags were scattered about. They looked through them all before one caught their eye. It was folded and had been on the floor under the whole pile amidst the dirt and filth that had accumulated over the years. Somehow, it had gone undetected. The pouch inside the bag had been pressed flat or nearly so, but it still contained nearly thirty ounces of nuggets. Tom and Twila were stunned and stood there in silence — tears streaming down their cheeks. For more than ten years they had kept their find a secret, but the $3500 from their honeymoon summer would never be forgotten. For them, it was literally the pot of gold at the end of the rainbow — a dream come true. But, in a way, it was a dream come true for us all. When we dare follow the tuggings in our hearts, no matter where they lead, it is quite possible to find ourselves in the eye of a rainbow.

On the morning of our seventh day on the tundra, Whitney and I awoke as usual and headed for the river. Our routine was as well established as the path we had created in this virgin place. Reduced to basics, our life was not a bad existence, but the strain was taking its toll.

We had long since stopped listening to the local radio station over the ADF and had turned off the ELT as well after the second day, when my friend Ofi managed to land on the gravel bar that had eluded us and had dropped off the food and tools we requested. There was bad weather all along the coast. When it cleared, we knew someone would come for us. They knew where we were.

It would have been nice had we not squandered all the food that same night that *Baldy Bird* was disassembled and trussed up for the helicopter lift off the mountain. We were to leave as well, we thought, the next day in the small airplanes that would come for us, and had celebrated with feasting and merriment on the life that was still ours — even though we still didn't understand the whys of it all and probably never would.

The river was our magnet. Without it, our time in this lonely, beautiful, desolate place would have been a grim tale. But instead, it had been a time to reflect and reevaluate and reconfirm the directions our lives had taken. There was no urgency to any of it. What would be would be. Neither of us would have traded places with anyone.

It was my turn to try to catch a fish and Whitney's to build the fire. Smoke was curling up through the willows that edged the sand bar we had adopted as our cooking area when Whitney heard the buzzing up the valley.

"Ted, it's a helicopter! Should I run up to *Baldy Bird* and get them on the radio?"

"You'd never make it in time, Whit. And besides, what frequency would they be on? Probably that geologist that Jack and I saw before." The sound soon faded.

The fishing was slow and Whitney's fire wasn't doing much better with all the soggy wood when all of a sudden, there it was again. Now we both could see it coming down the valley, straight for our smoke. It circled over our heads and settled on the gravel just out of blowing distance of the fire.

"They gave me the wrong coordinates. I've about used up all my fuel looking for you," yelled the pilot. It was Terry Eberle, the owner of Crystal Creek Lodge near Dillingham, who had come out in his own turbine-powered Hughes 500 to take us off the mountain. Our friends had been concerned with the way the weather was on the coast and had asked Terry if he could help.

"I haven't got much time. If you want a ride out of here, jump in now. I can barely make it back as it is."

Whitney ran to the fire and spilled the tea water on the flames (which had finally taken hold) while I pulled the fishing pole apart and climbed in beside Terry. Whitney was barely inside the back door when we lifted off and headed up the valley.

"I'm not very familiar with this part of the country," Terry said through the headsets as I reached for his chart on the console — an almost automatic reaction that I had developed early on. This was our first meeting.

"We could have gone back over the top the way I came, but the ceiling is coming down on us again. If you know a route through the mountain passes, I'm open for anything. We're going to be cutting it close!" he warned us once again.

As we wormed our way back through the rocky passes and to civilization once more, I was relieved that *Baldy Bird's* engine had died where it had. Even perfect technique would have spelled disaster here, and the humbleness that we experienced on the mountain came back again.

We had caused a lot of concern among our friends and those we cared about both near and far. My friend Denny was in route from Michigan to go on a wilderness fishing trip with me at season's end and was sitting in Anchorage, waiting for a plane change when he read in the newspaper that "Ted Mattson had crashed his Super Cub on a mountain somewhere between Bethel and Dillingham." My fishing buddies had cut the lock off my boat so he would have a place to stay while they tried to get us off the mountain.

Whitney had been able to get a message back to his parents, through Frank, so they wouldn't worry, but there had been no way to intercept his girlfriend, who was traveling and was to meet him at the airport in

Boise, Idaho in just two days. He would now just barely make it.

Terry Eberle refused to let me reimburse him for the hours he had put on his turbine helicopter and had even gone back out to the crash site and recovered the valuables we had left behind. He reluctantly accepted only two barrels of jet fuel for his efforts and the risk of using his $400,000 machine.

Baldy Bird came off the mountain a month later. It took a Huey to lift it, and there were some problems with it spinning and the bill was closer to $4000 than the $1500 estimate. By the time it was back in Palmer, I had spent nearly six grand and was still looking at another fifteen to get it flyable again. I sold it as is, but kept its clock so I would always have something from my old friend. I had thought for a while that flying might be out of my system once and for all, but it wasn't. Six months later, I bought *Baldy Bluebird*, a two-tone blue Super Cub who's fast becoming a friend as well.

What will I do next? I don't know. Maybe it's time I got a job. But then, some opal mines in Australia sure have been tugging at me lately.

Available from the Eddie Tern Press

*EYE OF THE RAINBOW An Alaskan Dream and Other
Tales* by Ted Mattson   Postpaid $14.00

*BURNING THE ICEBERG The Alaskan Fisherman's
Novel* by Whit Deschner   Postpaid $15.00

*HOW TO BE A JERK IN BRISTOL BAY An Abuser's
Guide* by Whit Deschner   Postpaid $11.00

*The Eddie Tern Press
HCR 88 Box 169
Baker OR 97814*